Ruth

Books in the Bible Study Commentary Series

BIBLE STUDY COMMENTARY

Ruth

PAUL P. ENNS

**ZONDERVAN
PUBLISHING HOUSE**
OF THE ZONDERVAN CORPORATION
GRAND RAPIDS, MICHIGAN 49506

Ruth: Bible Study Commentary
Copyright © 1982 by The Zondervan Corporation
Grand Rapids, Michigan

Library of Congress Cataloging in Publication Data

Enns, Paul P., 1937–
    Ruth: Bible study commentary.

    Bibliography: p.
    1. Bible. O.T. Ruth—Commentaries. I. Title.

BS1315.3.E56   1982   222'.3507   82-13500
ISBN 0-310-44061-0

Printed in the United States of America

83 84 85 86 87 88 — 10 9 8 7 6 5 4 3 2

To Jeremy

beloved son,

growing in grace

Contents

Ruth

Introduction

A. Title of the Book

The title for this book is derived from the principal character around whom the story centers. It is possible, although not certain, that the name Ruth means friendship or companionship.

In the Hebrew Bible the Book of Ruth is in the third division, the Writings, where it is grouped with the five Megilloth or scrolls. The other books included in the Megilloth are Song of Songs, Lamentations, Ecclesiastes, and Esther. Ruth was read at the Feast of Weeks (Pentecost) because of the emphasis in the book on the harvest.

In the Septuagint, the Latin Vulgate, and the English Bibles Ruth follows Judges because the events of Ruth occurred during the time of the judges.

B. Authorship

Although the Talmud suggests Samuel wrote the Book of Ruth, the intrinsic evidence suggests it was written after the death of Samuel. The mention of David in 4:22 infers it was not written earlier than David's reign, thereby excluding Samuel since he died prior to David's reign. However, since David is the last individual mentioned it also thereby suggests that the book was probably not written later than the time of David.

As with some other books of Scripture, the author of Ruth is unknown, nonetheless, the author wrote this beautiful narrative under the guidance of the Holy Spirit.

C. Date

There are a number of intrinsic statements that provide evidence for dating the book during the time of David:

1) Although the events of the story took place during the time of the judges, the writing of the book took place after the period of the judges. Keil and Delitzsch suggest an interval of 150 to 180 years between the events and the writing of the book.[1]

2) The explanation of the shoe custom in 4:7 also indicates a lapse of time between the period of the judges and the writing of Ruth. It does not, however, necessitate a late date for Ruth since the author seems to have a personal knowledge of the shoe custom. "He lived near enough to the change-over to remember what the previous custom was."[2]

3) The genealogy of 4:17–22 concludes with David, indicating a date during his reign. The mention of David's name indicates it could not have been written prior to his time; however, neither is it likely that it was written after his reign. Were that the case, Solomon's name could be expected. "Hence, the absence of Solomon's name seems to lend support to the view that the book was written sometime during the life of David the king."[3]

4) The language and style of Ruth are classical Hebrew and suggest an early date. Examples of archaic word forms abound. The idioms employed in the book also reflect an early period of Hebrew literary development.[4]

5) The presence of Aramaisms does not demand a late date for the book as liberal scholars suggest since Aramaisms were present in Palestine as early as the Amarna Age (14th century B.C.).[5]

[1]C. F. Keil and F. Delitzsch, *Joshua, Judges, Ruth* in *Biblical Commentary on the Old Testament* (Grand Rapids: William B. Eerdmans Publishing Co., 1968 reprint), p. 469.

[2]Arthur E. Cundall and Leon Morris, *Judges and Ruth* (Chicago: InterVarsity Press, 1968), p. 235.

[3]Edward J. Young, *An Introduction to the Old Testament* (Grand Rapids: William B. Eerdmans Publishing Co., 1964), p. 339.

[4]Cundall and Morris, *Judges and Ruth*, pp. 235–37.

[5]Roland Kenneth Harrison, *Introduction to the Old Testament* (Grand Rapids: William B. Eerdmans Publishing Co., 1969), p. 1061.

In addition, doubt remains whether the alleged words are in fact Aramaisms.

6) Some suggest the book was written in the postexilic era since it mentions a foreign woman becoming a member of Israelite society. However, this is unlikely since Ezra and Nehemiah rebuked the Jews for intermarriage (Ezra 9:1–10:44; Neh. 13:23–31). Ezra's concern was for the purity of the Jewish bloodline, and the story of Ruth would have had the opposite effect in the postexilic era.[6]

From the evidence it seems best to assign a date early in the reign of David (ca. 1000 B.C.) to the writing of Ruth.

D. Purpose

1. Boaz, as a kinsman-redeemer, serves as a type[7] of Jesus Christ. The analogy can readily be seen: 1) The kinsman-redeemer had to be a blood relative. Boaz was a relative of Ruth through Elimelech (2:1, 3, 20); Christ is a blood relative of the human race even though He was virgin born (John 1:14; Phil. 2:7–8; Heb. 2:14). 2) The kinsman-redeemer had to have the purchase price necessary to redeem his poor brother (cf. Lev. 25:25). Boaz was a wealthy man (2:1) who was able to purchase the land that belonged to Elimelech, Naomi's deceased husband, and marry Ruth to raise up a posterity for the deceased Elimelech (4:9–10). Because Christ was the sinless Son of God He was able to redeem a fallen human race (John 1:29; Isa. 53:5; 1 Peter 2:24). 3) The kinsman-redeemer had to be willing to redeem. Boaz was willing to buy back the forfeited property and marry Ruth (3:13; 4:9–10). Similarly, Christ willingly laid down His life to redeem the human race (Matt. 20:28; John 10:11, 17, 18; Heb. 10:9–10; 1 John 3:16).

2. There is a decided emphasis on Ruth as a foreigner (1:22; 2:2, 6, 10, 21; 4:5, 10). In this the Book of Ruth demonstrates that Gentiles are also within the scope of God's grace and bless-

---

[6]Harrison, p. 1061.

[7]For an important discussion of typology see Bernard Ramm, *Protestant Biblical Interpretation*, 3rd ed. (Grand Rapids: Baker Book House, 1970).

ing and the book also anticipates future Gentile blessing. Ruth, the Moabitess, became the great-grandmother of David (4:21–22) and the ancestor of Jesus Christ (Matt. 1:5, 16). As a Gentile Ruth was singularly blessed through her marriage to Boaz; in the millennial age the Gentile nations will be blessed through their identification with Israel (Isa. 2:3; 60:1–9; 66:18–21; Zech. 14:16).

3. There is clearly an emphasis on the genealogy of David, Israel's greatest king who is mentioned twice in the concluding verses (4:17, 22). The fact that the genealogy extends to David but no further also lends credence to this suggestion. Interestingly, David is the last word in the book.

4. The book also indicates that during a time of apostasy faith was still in existence. The period of the judges was a time of depravity, immorality, and anarchy, yet during this dark episode in Israel's history some still lived by faith in the Lord and in obedience to His revealed will. Ruth put herself under the authority of the Lord and His people (1:16–17); moreover, her virtue was well known (3:11). Boaz also demonstrated his obedience to the Lord in obeying the Levirate marriage law (3:12–13; 4:9–10; cf. Deut. 25:5–10).

E. Historical Background

The opening verse of the Book of Ruth identifies the events of the book as taking place "in the days when the judges ruled." The period of the judges covered more than three hundred years, from approximately 1390 B.C. until the rise of Saul in 1043 B.C. (cf. Judg. 11:26). The history of Israel at that time was marked by idolatry, immorality, and anarchy as the nation plunged into apostasy from the Lord. There were no leaders of the stature of Moses and Joshua, hence, any repentance was at best temporary. The chaotic condition of the period is described in Judges 21:25, "In those days Israel had no king; everyone did as he saw fit."

The Book of Ruth reveals a different aspect of the period as a godly Hebrew family leaves Israel for the land of Moab during a time of famine. However, in Moab the woman's husband and two sons die, leaving her alone with her Moabite daughters-in-law. One of them determines to remain with her mother-in-law and return with her to the land of Israel. Upon their return to Bethlehem the outworking of God's plan becomes evident as Ruth ingratiates herself with Boaz, a wealthy relative. Boaz subsequently fulfills the Levirate law by marrying Ruth and thereby becoming the kinsman-redeemer by protecting the inheritance of Naomi's deceased husband. The story comes to a successful conclusion as Ruth and Boaz become the grandparents of David, Israel's greatest king.

F. Outline of the Book

The book may be divided into four sections, following the chapter divisions within the book.

Chapter 1: Return of Ruth (1:1–22)
  A. Misfortune in Moab (1:1–5)
    1. Departure for Moab (1:1–2)
    2. Death of Naomi's husband (1:3)
    3. Death of Naomi's sons (1:4–5)
  B. Journey to Judah (1:6–18)
    1. Decision of Naomi (1:6–13)
    2. Decision of Orpah (1:14–15)
    3. Decision of Ruth (1:16–18)
  C. Misery of Mara (1:19–22)

Chapter 2: Reaping of Ruth (2:1–23)
  A. Field of Boaz (2:1–3)
  B. Provision of Boaz (2:4–17)
    1. Inquiry of Boaz (2:4–7)
    2. Instruction of Boaz (2:8–10)
    3. Intimation of Boaz (2:11–13)
    4. Invitation of Boaz (2:14–17)
  C. Reaction to Boaz (2:18–23)
    1. Blessing of Naomi (2:18–20)
    2. Benefit of Ruth (2:21–23)

Chapter 1

Return of Ruth
(Ruth 1:1–22)

The opening chapter of Ruth describes the dramatic events when Naomi, Elimelech, and their two sons migrated to Moab because of the famine in Judah. In Moab the two sons married Moabite women, but tragedy soon befell the family as Elimelech and the two sons died. Having heard that conditions were again favorable in Israel, Naomi determined to return to her homeland. In a beautiful depiction of faithfulness the remainder of the chapter records the decision of Ruth to return with Naomi and to serve Naomi's God.

A. Misfortune in Moab (1:1–5)

1. *Departure for Moab* (1:1–2)

It was during the dark days when the judges ruled that the events of the Book of Ruth took place. As mentioned previously, it was a time prior to the monarchy when there was no outstanding leader who was able to unite the nation; consequently, it was a period when everyone did as he saw fit (Judg. 21:25). The function of the judge was to "*act as law-giver, judge, governor* (giving law, deciding controversies and executing law, civil, religious, political, social; both early and late)."[1] The judges served in various capacities: in a legal sense in which they administered justice, in an administrative and leadership capacity,

---

[1]Francis Brown, S. R. Driver, and Charles A. Briggs, *A Hebrew and English Lexicon of the Old Testament* (Oxford: At the Clarendon Press, 1968), p. 1047.

as military leaders in delivering Israel from bondage to their oppressors, and as mediators of the true God.[2]

A famine of considerable magnitude engulfed the land of Canaan causing Elimelech and his family to migrate to the land of Moab. The severity of the famine is evident in that the family remained in Moab for about ten years (1:4). The time of the particular famine is indeterminable although the events described in Judges 6 are a plausible suggestion. The Midianites joined forces with the Amalekites to annually raid the Israelite crops and to devastate the land (Judg. 6:3–5). As a result the Israelites suffered severe losses and were impoverished (Judg. 6:6). The hardship and primitive lifestyle forced on the Israelites could be the background that caused Elimelech to leave the land (cf. Judg. 6:2).

Elimelech was from Bethlehem in Judah, so designated to distinguish it from Bethlehem of Zebulun (Josh. 19:15), a town of some prominence. Bethlehem may have suffered the effects of a drought sooner than some other locations since it lay in the Cenomanian Highlands, east of the water-parting.[3] This area would receive less rainfall than the land west of the central hill country ridge.

The land of Moab was a plateau rising to over 4000 feet and lying east of the Dead Sea between the Arnon and Zered rivers. The western area of Moab was fertile, receiving about sixteen inches of rainfall annually and was particularly suitable for grazing animals.

That Elimelech intended to remain in Moab temporarily is seen in the statement "went to live for a while" ("to sojourn," NASB; [Heb. *gēr*]).

> The root means to live among people who are not blood relatives; thus, rather than enjoying native civil rights, the *gēr* was dependent on the hospitality that played an important role in the

[2]For an amplified discussion see Paul P. Enns, *Judges: Bible Study Commentary* (Grand Rapids: Zondervan Publishing House, 1982), p. 9.

[3]Denis Baly, *The Geography of the Bible*, rev. ed. (New York: Harper & Row, Publishers, 1974), pp. 36, 54.

ancient near east. When the people of Israel lived with their neighbors they were usually treated as protected citizens; foreigners in Israel were largely regarded as proselytes.[4]

Earlier in Israel's history the patriarchs had also sojourned outside the land because of famine: Abraham had dwelt in Egypt (Gen. 12:10); Jacob also in Egypt (Gen. 47:4); Isaac in Gerar in the land of the Philistines (Gen. 26:1–3).

In the detailed account of the family journeying to Moab the writer provides the names of the family members—significant in the light of the story. The man's name was Elimelech meaning "God is King."

> Names in ancient times often reflected profound religious convictions, and this is one such. To name the name of God upon a child was to associate him in some way with God, and thus many Old Testament personal names include the name of the deity.[5]

The name Elimelech appears in the Amarna letters of the fourteenth century B.C. The wife of Elimelech was Naomi, whose name means "my pleasantness" or "my sweetness." Some suggest the name is derived from the Aramaic name Naaman meaning "my sweet one." The name is significant in the light of her name change in 1:20. The names of the two sons appears indicative of their physical weakness as the name Mahlon means "weakening" and Kilion means "pining."

The family members are termed Ephrathites since they were inhabitants of Ephrath, an ancient designation for Bethlehem (Gen. 35:19; 48:7; Mic. 5:2). The term is seen also as synonymous with Bethlehem in 4:11.

2. Death of Naomi's husband (1:3)

After an indeterminate period of time Elimelech died. It appears he did not live in Moab very long since the entire sojourn

---

[4]Harold G. Stigers, "גּוּר," *Theological Wordbook of the Old Testament*, R. Laird Harris, Gleason L. Archer, Jr., and Bruce K. Waltke, eds., vol. 1 (Chicago: Moody Press, 1980), vol. 1, p. 155.

[5]Arthur E. Cundall and Leon Morris, *Judges and Ruth* (Chicago: InterVarsity Press, 1968), p. 249.

of Naomi was ten years and the text suggests Mahlon and Kilion married after the death of their father and lived in Moab for some time after that. Elimelech is described as "Naomi's husband," suggesting at this point that Naomi would become a prominent personality in the story.

3. Death of Naomi's sons (1:4–5)

While living in Moab the sons of Naomi married Moabite women. Although Moabites were prohibited from entering into Israel's worship (Deut. 23:3–4), there was no explicit prohibition forbidding Israelites from intermarrying with Moabites. It is possible, however, that the injunction of Deuteronomy 7:3 would also relate to Moabites (although they are not mentioned in Deut. 7:1) since they were also an idolatrous people. It is also noteworthy that in the chronology of events the sons did not marry Moabite women until after the death of their father— suggesting the father would have disallowed the marriages. Some see the early deaths of Mahlon and Kilion as a judgment from the Lord, although as stated earlier, their names suggest they were sickly men.

The names of the Moabite women were Orpah and Ruth. A suggestion for the meaning of Orpah is "stiff-necked," suggestive of her refusal to return to Judah with her mother-in-law, but that is uncertain. The name Ruth may mean "friend" or "friendship," although the derivation of the name is also uncertain.

The dilemma of Naomi is portrayed in graphic fashion in 1:5 as she is left alone—separated from her husband and sons through their deaths. The widow's misfortune was serious as seen in the Scriptures (1 Kings 17:8–16; 2 Kings 4:1–7); as a result there is considerable emphasis in the Old Testament defending the widow (Deut. 10:18; 24:17–21; 26:12–13; 27:19; Isa. 1:23). God is seen as the widow's defender (Pss. 68:5; 146:9). In the New Testament James says, "Religion that God our Father accepts as pure and faultless is this: to look after orphans and widows in their distress and to keep oneself from being polluted by the world" (James 1:27).

B. Journey to Judah (1:6-18)

1. *Decision of Naomi* (1:6-13)

While in the land of Moab Naomi heard that the famine had ended in Judah and she resolved to return to her homeland where as a widow she could seek refuge with her relatives. Naomi portrays the oriental mind in recognizing that all events are ordained of the Lord for good or for ill. The sovereign purpose of God in history is also the emphasis of Scripture since He rules over all generations (Lam. 5:19; Ps. 103:19) and works out everything in conformity with the purpose of His will (Eph. 1:11).

Naomi heard that "the LORD had come to the aid of his people" (1:6). The translation "had come to the aid" is frequently translated "visited" (NASB, KJV). The term (*paqad*) may denote the gracious blessing and kindness of God or it may refer to punishment by the Lord and is frequently so translated (cf. Isa. 10:12; Jer. 6:15; 49:8; 50:31). In dealing with His elect people God has frequently visited them in blessing: the Lord fulfilled His promise to Sarah and Isaac was born (Gen. 21:1); the Lord ultimately delivered Israel from bondage in Egypt (Gen. 50:24, 25); He provided material blessings in nature (Ps. 65:9); He promised He would restore the Jews from Babylon (Jer. 27:22; 29:10; 32:5).

The Lord's chastisement of Israel had come to an end after ten years, and as a result the three women left the place where they had been living and set out for Judah (1:7). Although the three are pictured as leaving on the road to Judah, only Naomi is in view in the author's description of the return. The affection of the daughters for their mother-in-law is evident, however, as they accompany her.

Naomi was determined not to force her daughters-in-law into leaving their country and therefore urged each of them to return to her mother's home. The reference to "mother's home" is unusual since it was normal for a young woman to return to her father's home (Lev. 22:13; Num. 30:16; Judg. 19:2-3). Some suggest the reason for the return to their mother's home was that it was there they would receive consolation. A better suggestion seems to be that the mother's house "was the locus for matters pertinent to marriage, especially for discussion and planning for marriage"[6] (cf. Gen. 24:28; Song of Songs 3:4; 8:2). This would be consistent with Naomi's expression in verse 9 where she intimates they might be married again.

Naomi's parting concern for her daughters-in-law reveals that she had maintained a faith in Israel's God even though she lived in a foreign land where the people worshiped the heathen deities Astarte and Chemosh. Naomi expressed the earnest desire that Yahweh, the covenant God of Israel (Exod. 6:3) might bless them (1:8). Her desire was that the Lord would "show kindness" to her daughters-in-law. The word kindness (Heb. hesed) is an important Old Testament term. Nelson Glueck developed the thesis that hesed set forth the relationship of the Lord with Israel in His covenants with the nation. Glueck, and others who followed his thesis, suggested that the word did not so much emphasize mercy as loyalty to a covenant people when they fulfilled their obligation in the covenant. While this is certainly one emphasis of the term (cf. Exod. 20:6; 34:6, 7; Deut. 5:10; 7:9, 12) it is not the complete picture. Hesed must also be seen as involving the love and mercy of God as evidenced in Exodus 34:6-7 and other passages. Some passages emphasize the Lord's lovingkindness in providing redemption and forgiveness from sin (Num. 14:18-19; Ps. 103:8) and deliverance from trouble (Neh. 9:17). At times hesed is linked with nouns of mercy emphasizing the love of God (cf. Gen. 19:19; Exod. 34:6-7; Pss. 94:18-19; 103:4; 109:12; Zech. 7:9).

The word refers primarily to mutual and reciprocal rights and obligations between the parties of a relationship (especially Yahweh and Israel). But chesed is not only a matter of obligation; it is also of generosity. It is not only a matter of loyalty, but also of

---

[6]Edward F. Campbell, Jr., *Ruth* in *The Anchor Bible* (Garden City, N.Y.: Doubleday & Company, Inc., 1975), p. 64.

mercy. The weaker party seeks the protection and blessing of the patron and protector, but he may not lay absolute claim to it. The stronger party remains committed to his promise, but retains his freedom, especially with regard to the manner in which he will implement those promises. *Chesed* implies personal involvement and commitment in a relationship beyond the rule of law.[7]

It was essential to the young women that the Lord would show kindness to them because of the hardship of widowhood. The women had dealt kindly with their husbands; now Naomi prayed that the Lord would similarly show kindness to them.

Naomi's desire for her daughters-in-law was that they would find rest (cf. 3:1, translated "a home"; "security" in NASB) in the home of another husband. The word rest (Heb. *menuha*) may denote either the place or the state of rest. Here it denotes the "condition of rest and security attained by marriage";[8] ultimate rest will come in Messiah's millennial kingdom (Isa. 11:10).

In signaling her departure from them, Naomi kissed her daughters-in-law. In anticipation of the separation, the loud wailing, customary of eastern people, followed as the young women lamented the departure of Naomi (1:9). The affection of Ruth and Orpah toward Naomi is seen in their response: "We will go back with you to your people" (1:10). The negative is implied as in the NASB rendering, "*No*, but we will surely return. . . ." The response was unusual since a woman who had married a foreigner usually returned to her own people and her own gods upon the death of her husband.

Naomi recognized the futility of Ruth and Orpah accompanying her to Judah and dissuaded them from continuing with her. Both her concern and affection are revealed in her appeal: "Re-

---

[7]Merrill F. Unger and William White, Jr., *Nelson's Expository Dictionary of the Old Testament* (Nashville: Thomas Nelson Publishers, 1980), p. 232. For a helpful, detailed discussion see R. Laird Harris, "חֶסֶד," *Theological Wordbook*, vol. 1, pp. 305–7. See also Nelson Glueck, *Hesed in the Bible* (Hebrew Union College Press, 1967), and more recently a variant view by Katherine D. Sakenfeld, *The Meaning of Hesed in the Hebrew Bible* (Missoula, Mont.: Scholars Press, 1978).

[8]Brown, Driver, and Briggs, *Hebrew and English Lexicon*, p. 630.

turn home, my daughters (1:11); previously they were called daughters-in-law (1:8). Naomi reminded them that she was not pregnant and in fact could no longer bear children; hence, it would be futile for them to return with her. The law of the levirate marriage (Deut. 25:5–10) is in view in Naomi's words. She was unable to bear any more sons whom Ruth and Orpah could eventually marry and thereby raise up children to their deceased husbands. The levirate law (from the Latin, *levir*, meaning brother-in-law) specified that if a man died, having no son, his brother was to take the widow as his wife. When a son was born of this union, he was to assume the name of the dead brother that his name would not be blotted·out in Israel (Deut. 25:6). Thus the first son born was considered the son of the dead husband. However, if Ruth and Orpah returned with Naomi this levirate custom would not be fulfilled and they would have no opportunity for marriage. Naomi reinforced her appeal by reminding them that she was too old to have a husband (1:12).

In repeating the statement, "return home, my daughters" (1:12), Naomi followed her insistent plea by reminding Ruth and Orpah of the uselessness of accompanying her. The statement that follows cites three improbable conditions—each more unlikely than the preceding. Even if Ruth had hope (of still bearing children), even if she had a husband now, even if she gave birth to sons—would Ruth and Orpah remain unmarried and wait for the sons to grow up? No, they would not. The futility of accompanying Naomi was clear. The statement in Genesis 38:11 suggests that in some cases a younger son was obligated to wait until he was old enough to fulfill the levirate duty concerning a dead brother. In this case Tamar remained single until Shelah was old enough to fulfill his levirate duty as a brother of Er.

Naomi seems to suggest that Ruth and Orpah would get over their grief more readily than she since it was more bitter (Heb. *mārar*) for her than for them. The young women had lost their husbands but they would have opportunity to remarry; Naomi had lost not only her husband but also her two sons and would probably never remarry. The word bitter is an apt designation;

"the Hebrews expressed tragic, unpleasant experiences in terms of the sense of taste, the bitter . . . the more frequent use of *mar* is a figurative one, to express the emotional response to a destructive, heart-crushing situation."[9] Naomi's statement concerning her bitter experience anticipates 1:20.

Naomi's statement, "the LORD's hand has gone out against me" (1:13) reflects Eastern thinking.

> These concluding words arise from a conviction that underlies the whole of this book, namely, that things do not happen by chance. God is a sovereign God and He brings to pass what He will. Thus Naomi can ascribe responsibility for what has befallen her to no-one but Him.[10]

The designation "the LORD's hand" is a figure of speech known as anthropopatheia, and in this case denotes punishment.[11] The term is also used in a positive sense (cf. Isa. 11:11; John 10:28–29).

2. *Decision of Orpah* (1:14–15)

When Naomi concluded her exhortation for Ruth and Orpah to return to Moab the women wept again. Parting seemed imminent. There is a definite parallel between verses 9 and 14, yet also a contrast. In verse 9 Naomi kissed her daughters-in-law and the weeping followed. In verse 14 the weeping occurred first and the kissing followed. Moreover, in verse 9 Naomi took the initiative while in verse 14 Orpah kissed Naomi, suggesting the farewell and Orpah's return to Moab. "A one-way kiss of farewell is usual in stories of the conclusion of intimate relationships; cf. Gen. 31:28; 2 Sam. 19:40 (39); and 1 Kings 19:20."[12]

The terse statement, "but Ruth clung to her," sets Ruth in contrast to Orpah. While Ruth's faithfulness and insistence on remaining with Naomi is evident, Orpah was nonetheless obe-

---

[9]Victor P. Hamilton, "מָרַר," *Theological Wordbook*, vol. 1, p. 529.

[10]Cundall and Morris, *Judges and Ruth*, p. 258.

[11]E. W. Bullinger, *Figures of Speech Used in the Bible* (Grand Rapids: Baker Book House, 1968), p. 879.

[12]Campbell, *Ruth*, p. 72.

dient to Naomi in returning to her people. The statement, "Ruth clung" (Heb. *dābaq*), is expressive. "Used in modern Hebrew in the sense of 'to stick to, adhere to,' *dābaq* yields the noun form for 'glue' and also the more abstract ideas of 'loyalty, devotion.'"[13] The concluding words of verse 14 emphasize the loyalty of Ruth in adamantly remaining with her mother-in-law.

Naomi made a final appeal to Ruth to return to her people, reminding her that her sister-in-law was returning to her people and her gods.[14] The designation "her people" does not refer to her family but to the land of Moab; she was returning to her nation. The term "her gods" indicates that deities were associated with a particular nation (cf. Judg. 10:6). Chemosh was the prominent god of the Moabites (Num. 21:29; Judg. 11:24), although the female goddess Astarte was worshiped in conjunction with Chemosh. It appears the worship of Chemosh involved the sacrificial offering of children (cf. 2 Kings 3:27). Chemosh was not only considered the god of warfare, but also the provider of the necessities of life.

3. *Decision of Ruth* (1:16–18)

Although Orpah returned to her people, Ruth exhibited a great love and devotion to her mother-in-law for she determined to go with Naomi, howbeit at great personal sacrifice. Naomi had been pleading with the two women to return to Moab but Ruth asked Naomi to refrain. Following that Ruth uttered her well-known statement. In Ruth's fourfold statement she indicated her desire to follow Naomi to Bethlehem and adopt her people and her God. Although the word lodge (Heb. *lîn*) normally means to spend the night (cf. Judg. 19:13, 15), in this context it denotes permanence. Ruth was leaving the Moabites permanently in order to identify herself with Naomi's people. The final two phrases of verse 16 indicate that Ruth's decision was both social and religious. She was adopting the Hebrew people as her own

---

[13] Unger and White, *Nelson's Expository Dictionary*, p. 61.

[14] The Hebrew word for God (Elohim) is a plural form and should probably be translated as a plural in this case since the Moabites were polytheistic.

people and the Hebrews' God as her God. The statement of Ruth stands in contrast to Orpah's action in verse 15. While Orpah returned to her people and her gods Ruth adopted Naomi's people as her people and Naomi's God as her God. Ruth's action was deliberate since 1:17 and 2:12 indicate that she was not uninformed concerning Israel's God.

Ruth concluded her solemn statement by vowing that even death would not separate her from Naomi and her people (v. 17). The words "Where you die I will die, and there I will be buried" emphasize this truth. It is interesting to note that in the accounts describing the death of the patriarchs the emphasis is on "died" and "buried" and being gathered to their own people (cf. Gen. 25:8-9; 35:29, etc.). Those who had adopted the true God of Israel would not be separated even in death. Hence, out of a common belief families had their own burial places (Gen. 47:30; 49:29).

> Sufficient archaeological data is now available concerning burial practices in Palestine in biblical times to show how it can be said that people are not separated even by death. Family tombs were the dominant feature, and after decomposition of the flesh was complete, bones were gathered in a common repository in the tomb, either in an ossuary or in a pit cut out of the rock in the floor of the tomb. A body might be placed in the tomb to decompose, or, if the family member died at some distance from home, the body could be interred at the distant spot and then the bones gathered up several months later for transport to the family tomb and deposit in the repository (cf. 2 Sam. 21:10–14).[15]

Ruth solemnized her determination with an oath involving the Lord's judgment of death on her if anything except death itself would separate her from Naomi and her people. The oath formula of verse 17 is found eleven times in the books of Samuel and Kings. It is thought that the oath was accompanied by a symbolic gesture across the throat with a finger. The oath is used similarly in 1 Samuel 20:13 where Jonathan affirms his friend-

---

[15]Campbell, *Ruth*, pp. 74–75.

ship with David by an oath of death if he should fail to warn David of Saul's intentions against him (cf. also 1 Sam. 25:22, 1 Kings 20:10; 2 Kings 6:31).

It is noteworthy that Ruth invoked the name of the Lord (commonly translated Yahweh) in her oath; it indicated Ruth's adoption of Israel's covenant God as her God for Gentiles always used Elohim in swearing an oath. Ruth had come to faith in the Lord and was therefore identifying herself forever with the Lord's people.

The resoluteness of Ruth is seen in the words "was determined" in verse 18. The word determined (Heb. *'āmēs*) in its root means to be stout, strong, bold, alert and here means to "confirm oneself in a purpose, be determined."[16] The verb is reflexive and emphasizes the fact that Ruth strengthened herself in this resolve. Recognizing Ruth's determination, Naomi refrained from further urging her to remain with the Moabite people.

C. Misery of Mara (1:19-22)

Although the details of the journey from Moab to Bethlehem are not described, the journey had to have been arduous. Traveling north to skirt the Dead Sea, the duo descended from the heights of Moab into the Jordan Rift Valley which lies 1,290 feet below sea level at the point where the Jordan River flows into the Dead Sea. Crossing the lush area of the Jordan bed known as the *Zor* they began the ascent of the *Ghor*, the rugged desert region that stretched up to fifteen miles in width.[17] The journey took them to Bethlehem, a town six miles south of Jerusalem, lying more than 2300 feet above sea level in the hill country of Judah.

The excitement of the people of Bethlehem at the return of Naomi is evident from the statement in verse 19: "the whole town was stirred because of them." The verb "stirred" (Heb.

---

[16]Brown, Driver, and Briggs, *Hebrew and English Lexicon*, pp. 54–55.

[17]See discussion by Yohanan Aharoni, *The Land of the Bible* (Philadelphia: The Westminster Press, 1967), p. 31.

hûm) means to murmur, roar, or disturb greatly and emphasizes the great excitement and gossip surrounding Naomi's return. The same word is used to describe the excitement of the Israelites when the ark was brought into the camp (1 Sam. 4:5). The feminine form "they said" (translated "the women" in NASB, NIV) indicates it was the women in the town who were excited.

The question "Can this be Naomi?" may suggest excitement and happiness at the return of a member of the community but may also express amazement that she had returned without her husband and sons.

As the women greeted Naomi by her name, "Pleasant," (see verse 2) she responded in remorse, "Don't call me Naomi, call me Mara, because the Almighty has made my life very bitter" (v. 20). The statement is a play on words regarding her name. She no longer wanted to be known as "Pleasant," but rather Mara, meaning bitter, because the Almighty had made her life very bitter. Naomi refers to God as Almighty (Heb. *Shadday*), a name for God found forty-eight times in the Old Testament, thirty-one times in the Book of Job. The most common translation for *Shadday* has been Almighty and is also the thought of the Latin Vulgate translation *omnipotens*. The origin of the name is unclear and many suggestions have been offered. A common older view is that *Shadday* is derived from the Hebrew verb *shadad*, "to destroy," and thereby refers to God as "My Destroyer." A more recent suggestion relates the name to the Akkadian *šadu*, meaning mountain, so that God was revealed in His mighty power in the mountain phenomena such as volcanic eruptions or simply the strength that the mountain denoted. A derivitive of this would be references that depict God as a "rock." The identification of *Shadday* with mountain is the most common explanation today. Still other suggestions relate the name to the Sumerian *sazu*, meaning that God is All-knowing or that the name is derived from the word used in Scripture for a woman's breast, hence, God is known as God All-sufficient. Morris provides an excellent summary of the usage of the name. In examining the patriarchal passages where the term is used he concludes, "In each of these passages there is the thought of the power of God. He disposes as He sees fit, and no obstacle need be taken into account." In examining the other passages he concludes:

> From all this it seems that the thought of power does attach to the name. There are many passages wherein this is the most appropriate meaning, and very few, if any, where it is not acceptable. We should accordingly take this to be the basic force of *šadday* as a name of God.[18]

Naomi recognized that the events of life were not the product of chance but the design of a sovereign God almighty. Her negative understanding of God's sovereign dealing was similar to Job (Job 6:4). Naomi was unaware that while the present was a bitter experience to her, the outworking of God's sovereign plan would result in blessing and joy to her and Ruth in the present, and in the future to all people through Jesus Christ who would come from the lineage of Boaz and Ruth (4:13–17).

Naomi's bitterness is explained in verse 21. She went away full—with husband and two sons, but returned empty—she lost her husband and both sons; she was destitute. The final statement of verse 21 may read either "the LORD has afflicted me" or "the LORD has testified against me." The former appears more suitable since it both fits the context and also forms a parallelism in the statement. In Hebrew poetry meter rather than rhyme is the emphasis. One example of Hebrew poetry is synonymous parallelism in which the second line repeats the thought of the first line using different words, hence, the phrase "the Almighty has brought misfortune upon me" repeats the thought expressed in "The LORD has afflicted me."

---

[18]Cundall and Morris, *Judges and Ruth*, pp. 266–67. Morris provides a very helpful discussion on both the origin and usage of the term. See also Victor P. Hamilton, "שַׁדַּי," *Theological Wordbook*, vol. 2, p. 907; Unger and White, *Expository Dictionary*, pp. 159–60; H. B. Kuhn, "God, Names of," *The Zondervan Pictorial Encyclopedia of the Bible*, Merrill C. Tenney, gen. ed., vol. 2 (Grand Rapids: Zondervan Publishing House, 1975), p. 763; Helmer Ringgren, *Israelite Religion* (Philadelphia: Fortress Press, 1966), p. 22.

Verse 22 is a transitional statement in that it concludes the first segment of the narrative in which Naomi and her family have sojourned in Moab, but now, upon the death of her husband and two sons, she has returned to her native town in Judah with Ruth her Moabite daughter-in-law. The mention of the barley harvest emphasizes the transitional statement in that it anticipates the events that follow. The barley harvest took place in late April or early May, about a month earlier than the wheat harvest (cf. Exod. 9:31–32). Barley was cheaper than wheat and thus an important crop that was used in feeding cattle. It became the food of poor people (cf. John 6:9), and since it was a staple in Israel, the nation was symbolized by barley bread (Judg. 7:13). The first fruits of the harvest were presented to the Lord (Lev. 23:10–11).

For Further Study

1. Read an article on Moab in a Bible dictionary or encyclopedia. Study the topography as well as the history of the land.

2. Develop a concordance study on the term widow. What does Scripture emphasize concerning widowhood? (Cf. Ps. 146:9; Isa. 1:17; James 1:27.)

3. Read an article on Bethlehem in a Bible dictionary or encyclopedia.

4. What are the implications of the name of God almighty for the believer?

Chapter 2

Reaping of Ruth
(Ruth 2:1–23)

Chapter 2 describes the sovereign provision of God for Naomi and Ruth as they arrived in Judah at the time of the barley harvest. The story introduces the reader to Boaz, the close relative of Naomi, and the kinsman-redeemer, who became the provision and instrument for blessing for Naomi and Ruth. As Ruth began to glean among the sheaves she encountered Boaz who exceeded the demands of the law in providing for Ruth.

A. Field of Boaz (2:1–3)

In anticipation of his meeting with Ruth, Boaz is described in verse 1. He is identified as a "relative on her husband's side," literally, an acquaintance or one who is known. The text indicates Boaz was a relative of Elimelech, the deceased husband of Naomi, and he is further described as a close relative and kinsman-redeemer (2:20).

Boaz is also described as "a man of standing," a phrase combining two Hebrew words, *gibbor ḥayil*. The word *gibbor* means "a particularly strong or mighty person who carries out, can carry out, or has carried out great deeds, and surpasses others in doing so."[1] A usual translation, therefore, is "hero," especially with respect to military service. The word emphasizes

---

[1]H. Kosmala, "גָּבַר," *Theological Dictionary of the Old Testament*, G. Johannes Botterweck and Helmer Ringgren, eds., John T. Willis, trans. rev. ed., vol. 2 (Grand Rapids: William B. Eerdmans Publishing Co., 1977), p. 373.

an individual who is exceptionally important or powerful in some particular field. The word *hayil* may mean "strength (general, of a warrior, of military forces), ability (in war and in some vocation), or wealth (possessions)."[2] Thus in Ruth 2:1 it indicates a rich landowner. The most frequent use of the word *gibbor* is with respect to military activities and military prowess, denoting one who is "eligible for military service or is able to bear arms, or one who has actually fought in combat, who has already distinguished himself by performing heroic deeds."[3] Interestingly, the word *gibbor* is also used in combination with *el* (God) as a title of Messiah in Isaiah 9:6 where *el gibbor* is translated "Mighty God." This takes on particular significance since Boaz is seen as a type of Christ and the same word that is used to describe the prominent status of Boaz in Ruth 2:1 is also used as a title of Christ in Isaiah 9:6.

The meaning of the name Boaz is uncertain. A commonly accepted meaning has been "in him is strength," which would have particular significance for Ruth as he was her kinsman-redeemer. Recently some have suggested the name comes from an Arabic root meaning "quickness."

Ruth asked permission of Naomi to go into the fields to pick up the leftover grain after the farmers had completed their harvesting. Ruth is termed "the Moabitess," an emphasis by the writer (1:22; 2:2, 21; 4:5, 10) that ultimate blessing through the birth of the great king David (4:17) and Christ (Matt. 1:5) would be through a foreigner.

Ruth's earlier mention of the Lord, the covenant God of Israel, indicated that she had a knowledge of the true God. This may be further reflected in her request, for the law of Moses provided for the poor to pick up leftover grain in the fields. This was God's provision for the poor. For example, the reapers were not to reap to the very edges of their fields, nor were they to pick up sheaves that had been dropped; they were to be left for the

---

[2]Kosmala, "גָּבַר," *Theological Dictionary*, vol. 2, p. 374.
[3]Kosmala, "גָּבַר," *Theological Dictionary*, vol. 2, p. 374.

alien, orphan, or widow (Lev. 19:9; 23:22; Deut. 24:19). However, since not all landowners responded graciously toward
those in need, Ruth determined to pick up the leftover grain in
the field of one "in whose eyes I find favor," that is, one who
would permit her to do so.

With Naomi's permission Ruth departed and "As it turned
out, she found herself working in a field belonging to Boaz"
(v. 3). The phrase "as it turned out" (Heb. *miqreh*) is important
in seeing the sovereign hand of God in the affair. Left to her own
choice, Ruth could have picked up grain in any field, but God
determined that she would pick up grain in a specific field—that
belonging to Boaz, in order that God's sovereign purpose might
be accomplished in the outworking of the events. The use of this
word indicates that "divine providence is the cause . . . nothing
happens by chance, or fate. God controls all."[4] The renewed
reminder that Boaz was from the clan of Elimelech points to
Boaz' eligibility as the kinsman-redeemer. God's sovereign purpose is being effected!

B. Provision of Boaz (2:4–17)

1. Inquiry of Boaz (2:4–7)

As Boaz arrived at the harvest field from Bethlehem he
greeted the reapers with the customary salutation, "The LORD
be with you!" The reapers responded with a similar benediction.
Boaz' statement indicates his spiritual piety and is also a reminder that the Hebrews assimilated God into all of life's experiences (cf. Ps. 129:8). When Boaz noticed Ruth he inquired of the
foreman, "Whose young woman is that?" (v. 5). The foreman
(Heb. *na'ar*) had the responsibility of superintending the opera-
tions in the harvest field, supplying provisions to the reapers,
and paying them for their work at the end of the day.[5] The
question about the identity of the young woman (Heb. *na'arah*)

---

[4]Carl Schultz, "קָרָה," *Theological Wordbook*, vol. 2, p. 814.

[5]Robert Jamieson, "Ruth," *A Commentary Critical, Experimental, and
Practical on the Old and New Testaments* (Grand Rapids: William B. Eerdmans
Publishing Co., 1945 reprint), p. 130.

is purposeful in that it probes the circumstances and moves the story forward.[6]

The servant responded to Boaz by informing him that the young woman was a Moabitess who had returned from Moab with Naomi. In verse 7 the foreman rehearses Ruth's request in his explanation to Boaz. Ruth's request was unusual in that she asked, "Please let me glean and gather among the sheaves behind the harvesters" (v. 7). The harvesters cut the grain with their sickles while the female workers followed, binding the cut grain into sheaves. Ruth's request was that she might follow the harvesters and gather up any grain that had fallen from the sheaves that had been prepared for binding. This would have been an unusual privilege (v. 15).

The foreman continued to explain, emphasizing Ruth's diligence. She had come out to the field early in the morning and had worked steadily apart from a brief rest she took in the shelter. The word shelter literally reads house but could hardly refer to Ruth's own house, nor would she have been in Boaz' house. The word probably refers to the shelter such as a tent that enabled the workers to rest and refresh themselves.

2. *Instruction of Boaz* (2:8–10)

Upon hearing about the young Moabitess, Boaz responded with generosity toward Ruth and made her task easier. This is all the more unusual since the gleaners would not always have been treated favorably. Boaz' address, "My daughter," suggests he may have been considerably older than Ruth. He asked her to listen to him and urged her not to leave his field in order to glean in other fields. The indication is that gleaners would move about from one field to another in order to find more grain. Boaz urged Ruth to remain with the women who were working in his field. But gleaning this close to the harvesters could result in harassment from the men; hence, Boaz reminded Ruth that he had commanded the men not to touch her, ensuring her safety. Boaz

[6]Campbell, *Ruth*, pp. 93–94.

granted her further privileges. Ruth was given permission to drink water from the jars that the servants brought to the field for the workers. It would not have been customary to provide water for the gleaners, but this act was a further demonstration of the kindness of Boaz toward Ruth.

Ruth was overwhelmed by the beneficence of Boaz and "bowed down with her face to the ground" (v. 10). Just as the generosity and kindness of Boaz has been evident, so the humility of Ruth is also seen. The verb "to bow down" (*shāchāh*) is usually used to denote homage before a king or a superior. It is also used in worshiping the Lord (e.g., 1 Sam. 15:25), but in this instance it emphasizes Ruth's humility (cf. 1 Sam. 25:23; 2 Sam. 1:2). Ruth was amazed that Boaz should favor her in this way since she was a foreigner, and as such, she had no privileges in a foreign land.

3. *Intimation of Boaz* (2:11–13)

Boaz knew all about Ruth's devotion and loyalty to her mother-in-law: "I've been told all about what you have done for your mother-in-law since the death of your husband." There is no indication that Ruth had spoken to anyone of her sacrifice; indeed, the information would have come from Naomi herself, particularly since Boaz was a near relative. Boaz emphasized that he had received a *full* report of Ruth's sacrifice. The same expression is found in Joshua 9:24 where the Gibeonites reminded Joshua that they had been fully informed of the Israelites' instruction by the Lord to destroy all the inhabitants of the land.[7]

Boaz was fully aware of the supreme sacrifice of Ruth—she had left all that was important to her—father, mother, and homeland. There could be no greater sacrifice. Morris draws an interesting parallel between Ruth's venture of faith and that of the patriarch, Abraham.

---

[7]The infinite absolute adds emphasis when preceding the finite verb, thus, "has been *fully* told me." Cf. A. R. S. Kennedy, *The Book of Ruth, The Hebrew Text with Grammatical Notes and Vocabulary* (London: Society for Promoting Christian Knowledge, 1928), p. 34.

Ruth, like the patriarch, went out not knowing whither she went. And like Abraham she trusted Yahweh. Again, Abraham was accompanied only by his wife who was designated "barren" . . . Yet God in a wonderful way was to give them a child, and God in a wonderful way was to give Ruth a child.[8]

Ruth, like Abraham, had left her heathen background and country and came to the Land of Promise, the place of God's blessing.

In the light of Ruth's faithfulness, Boaz prayed that the Lord would reward her in full measure even as Abraham had been rewarded before her (Gen. 15:1). The reward to Abraham would be an heir through which the Abrahamic covenant would one day be fulfilled (Gal. 3:16); the reward to Ruth would be similar—through her lineage the Messiah would ultimately come (Matt. 1:5). Ironically, it was through Boaz who prayed that God would ultimately answer the prayer (4:13–17).

In graphic imagery Boaz compared Ruth's sojourn to Judah to taking refuge under the wings of God (2:12). Attributing wings to God is an anthropopatheia, also termed an anthropomorphism, which denotes God's care[9] (cf. Deut. 32:11; Pss. 36:7; 57:1; 91:4). The figure illustrates a young eagle seeking refuge under the wings of its mother, finding security and shelter. Craigie expands the illustration in his comment on Deuteronomy 32:11:

> Apparently the eagle taught its young to fly by throwing one out of the nest, and then swooping down and allowing the young bird to alight on its mother's wings. The poetry illustrates vividly God's dealings but remaining beneath them to give them strength for the fearful experience, and gradually teaching them to "fly" on their own.[10]

Ruth expressed her gratitude toward Boaz. The statement

---

[8]Cundall and Morris, *Judges and Ruth*, p. 276.

[9]E. W. Bullinger, *Figures of Speech Used in the Bible* (Grand Rapids: Baker Book House, 1968 reprint), p. 895.

[10]P. C. Craigie, *The Book of Deuteronomy* in *The New International Commentary on the Old Testament* (Grand Rapids: William B. Eerdmans Publishing Co., 1976), p. 381.

"May I continue to find favor" both expresses Ruth's thankful-
ness and her confidence about future well-being.[11] A similar
expression is found in 1 Samuel 1:18 in Hannah's statement to
Eli. Ruth had received comfort (Heb. *nehāmâ*) from Boaz. The
same word occurs in Isaiah 40:1 in comforting the Jews living in
exile in Babylon; they would find comfort in their return to the
land through the decree of Cyrus. The parallel is interesting for
Ruth also finds comfort upon her entrance into the land. The
same Hebrew word is used in Psalm 23:4, where David finds
comfort under the protective care of the Good Shepherd.

The second phrase of 2:13 may explain the comfort, namely,
Ruth was comforted because Boaz had spoken kindly, literally
stated, "You have . . . spoken kindly to [the heart of your] servant." Boaz' words had touched Ruth's heart. Ruth's humility is
revealing in the statement as she refers to herself as a servant
(*shiphâ*). Some suggest this expression is a more demeaning
term than the word Ruth uses in 3:9 (*āmāh*). In any case, Ruth
clearly evidences humility as she recognizes her unworthy estate
and all she receives from Boaz is due to his gracious benevolence.

4. *Invitation of Boaz* (2:14–17)

Boaz was clearly impressed with Ruth's humility and at meal-
time he invited her to eat with the harvesters. Boaz summoned
her, "Come over here," literally, "draw near," which suggests
Ruth's modesty. Boaz invited Ruth to partake of the bread and
dip it in the wine vinegar. The wine vinegar (Heb. *hōmes*) was
produced through the fermentation of alcoholic liquids, primarily wine. It was a forbidden drink for those under the Nazirite
vow (Num. 6:3) and is the drink mentioned in the prophecy of
Christ on the cross (Ps. 69:21). In the latter passage as well as in
the fulfillment in the New Testament (Luke 23:36) the wine
vinegar is used in a negative sense. The wine vinegar was sometimes diluted and used for dipping morsels of bread which

---

[11]Campbell, *Ruth*, p. 100.

proved to be a thirst-quenching refreshment.[12] Sometimes olive oil was added to the wine vinegar, and this also used as a relish with bread.

When Ruth joined the harvesters at Boaz' request he also offered her some roasted grain (Heb. *qālî*). The preparation of the grain was as follows:

> a quantity of the best ears, not too ripe, are plucked with the stalks attached. These are tied into small parcels, a blazing fire is kindled with dry grass and thorn bushes, and the cornheads are held in it until the chaff is mostly burned off. The grain is thus sufficiently roasted to be eaten, and is a favourite article all over the country.[13]

The sufficiency of Boaz' provision is seen in the statement, "She ate all she wanted and had some left over" (v. 14), enabling her to bring some to Naomi.

But when Ruth rose to leave, Boaz provided for her future needs as well by instructing the men to allow Ruth to gather grain from among the sheaves; moreover, they were to pull out stalks from among the bundles for Ruth to pick up (2:15–16). Boaz' protective care for Ruth is evident as he had previously instructed the men not to touch her (v. 9); now he again gave orders to the men not to embarrass her (v. 15). The privilege of Ruth as well as her status as a foreign woman no doubt made the warning to the men necessary. It was abnormal for a gleaner to pick up grain close to the harvesters. They were normally permitted to glean only after the harvesters had completed their work; furthermore, since she was a Moabitess, she would be more susceptible to insult and embarrassment, hence the warning of Boaz. The word embarrass (Heb. *kelimmâ*) may denote any kind of public disgrace as seen in the Arabic cognate which means "to wound."[14] It may also mean an improper advance that would cause embarrassment, thus Boaz' warning.

---

[12]D. Kellerman, "חֹמֶץ," *Theological Dictionary*, vol. 4, pp. 487–93.
[13]Cundall and Morris, *Judges and Ruth*, p. 278.
[14]J. N. Oswalt, "כְּלִמָּה," *Theological Wordbook*, vol. 1, p. 443.

Not only were the harvesters to allow Ruth to gather grain among the sheaves (v. 15), but they were to pull out stalks of grain from the bundles for Ruth to glean. "Pull out some stalks" refers to a handful—the amount of grain grasped with the left hand as the sickler cuts it with his right hand.[15] A further prohibition followed: "don't rebuke her" (v. 16). This was a serious warning that the harvesters were not to prevent Ruth from acquiring what Boaz had provided for her.

Verse 17 is a summary statement that explains the results of Boaz' benevolence to Ruth. She continued gathering grain until evening when she took her yield and threshed it. Threshing a small amount of grain involved beating it with a curved stick. A parallel is found in Gideon beating out the wheat in the winepress (Judg. 6:11). Larger amounts were threshed by oxen pulling heavy sledges studded with metal or stones. When Ruth finished threshing she had an ephah of barley—about one half bushel, which would have weighed about thirty pounds.

C. Reaction to Boaz (2:18–23)

1. *Blessing of Naomi* (2:18–20)

After the successful day of gathering grain Ruth carried the thirty pounds of barley into town and her mother-in-law saw the large amount of grain that Ruth had gathered. The indication is that Naomi was astonished at the quantity of grain since this would have been unusual for gleaners. Because of Naomi's poverty, the barley was a great blessing and cause for rejoicing. In addition to the large yield, Ruth gave Naomi what she had left over after she had eaten and was fully satisfied (v. 18). The phrase "she had eaten enough" (Heb. *sāb'â*) emphasizes that Ruth was satiated and indicates the abundant provision of Boaz for Ruth. He had provided more than enough for her, enabling her to share of her abundance with Naomi. The verb form is used in Exodus 16:8 in describing God's full provision for Israel in the wilderness by supplying them with manna and quails.

---

[15]Campbell, *Ruth*, p. 104.

Naomi's astonishment is reflected in her staccato questions and her praise of Ruth's benefactor (v. 19). The two questions, "Where did you glean today? Where did you work?" should not be understood as suggesting that Ruth had labored in two different places. Rather, this is an example of Hebrew poetry called synonymous parallelism in which the second line repeats the thought of the first line in slightly different words. Naomi concluded her questions with a blessing on the one who had dealt so bountifully with Ruth—although he still remained unknown to Naomi. The term blessed (Heb. *bārak*) is used frequently in the Old Testament.

> (Blessing) was primarily a prayer for the Lord's presence, grace, and keeping power. It was summed up in the expression "they shall put my name upon the children of Israel," i.e. God himself would be their God (Num 6:23–27). . . . Its major function seems to have been to confer abundant and effective life upon something (Gen. 2:3; 1 Sam. 9:13; Isa. 66:3) or someone (Gen. 27:27f.; Gen. 49). . . . This address becomes a formalized means of expressing thanks and praise to this person because he has given out of the abundance of his life.[16]

In a blessing bestowed by God three fundamental aspects are distinguishable:

> (a) It consists in numerous offspring; "be fruitful and multiply" says Elohim to the first men after having blessed them (Gen. 1:28; 9:1); this is also the basic element of the blessing given to Abraham (Gen. 12:1; 13:16) and David receives the promise that his dynasty will be eternal (2 Sam. 7:29). (b) Riches are the second sign of blessing: the blessed man has many possessions (Gen. 24:35). Job is an example of a man blessed by a large posterity and abundant wealth, and one of the closing chapters of Deuteronomy similarly expresses the constant connection between blessing and prosperity (Dt. 28:1–13). (c) Blessing finally consists in being victorious over one's enemies, as appears from

---

[16]J. N. Oswalt, "בָּרַךְ," *Theological Wordbook*, vol. 1, p. 285.

many texts belonging to the heroic age of the early tribes (Gen. 27:29; 49:8–12, 22–26; Dt. 28:7).[17]

Rather than answering Naomi's questions, Ruth responded by referring to the one whom Naomi had blessed. His name was Boaz! When Naomi discovered that it was her relative Boaz who had shown kindness to Ruth, she pronounced her blessing on him once more, "The LORD bless him!" (v. 20). But it was more than Boaz' act of kindness; Naomi saw the beneficence of a sovereign God accomplishing His purpose through Boaz. Naomi recognized the Lord's kindness (Heb. *ḥesed,* see discussion at 1:8) "to the living and the dead." The living refers to Naomi and Ruth while the dead refers to Naomi's deceased husband and sons. While the immediate kindness to Ruth and Naomi was in the provision of barley, it is possible that Naomi recognized that the law of the kinsman-redeemer would ultimately be enacted, thereby preserving the name of the dead.[18]

Naomi reminded Ruth that Boaz was a close relative and a kinsman-redeemer. The word kinsman-redeemer (Heb. *gō'ēl*) merits careful study since it is the significant term in the Book of Ruth. The primary idea of the word is a kinsman rescuing or redeeming a relative from trouble. It stands as basically synonymous for the Hebrew word *pādhāh,* meaning to ransom, as it is used in Isaiah 35:10 where those ransomed of the Lord will enter the millennial kingdom with joy. It is also parallel to *hoshia',* meaning to save or deliver, and is used of the joyful worship in Jerusalem during the millennial kingdom in Isaiah 60:16. The name of Jesus is a derivative of this word.

The kinsman-redeemer was a close relative such as a brother, uncle, cousin, or other relative who would defend the rights of the person and help him or her in a time of trouble. The

[17]Edmond Jacob, *Theology of the Old Testament* (New York: Harper & Row, 1958), p. 179; see also Josef Scharbert, "ברך," *Theological Dictionary of the Old Testament,* vol. 2, pp. 279–308.

[18]Louise Pettibone Smith, "The Book of Ruth," in *The Interpreter's Bible,* George Arthur Buttrick, ed. (New York: Cokesbury Press, 1953), vol. 2, p. 843.

kinsman-redeemer served in a variety of ways: 1) If an Israelite became so poor that he had to sell his property the kinsman-redeemer was to buy back the property and restore it to the family (Lev. 25:23–34). The reason appears to be given in Leviticus 25:23. The land all belonged to the Lord; the Israelites were merely stewards of the Lord's possession, hence, the land was not to be sold permanently but was to remain within the family. It is this aspect that applies to the Book of Ruth as Boaz became willing to not only buy the property but also to marry Ruth, which idea apparently was derived from the levirite law in Deuteronomy 25:5–10 (although the term *gō'ēl* is not mentioned in the passage). 2) If an Israelite became indebted to another man (presumably a foreigner) that he sold himself as a slave to the man, then the Israelite was to have the right of redemption, whereby a near relative could redeem him by paying the purchase price (Lev. 25:47–55). 3) If an Israelite was murdered, his near relative was to be the kinsman-redeemer by avenging the blood of his relative. As the "avenger of blood" he had the responsibility of killing the murderer (cf. Num. 35:12–27; Deut. 19:6). 4) God is seen as the redeemer of Israel: He redeems the fatherless and widows (Prov. 23:11); He redeemed Israel through the Exodus (Pss. 74:2; 106:10); He redeemed Israel from Babylon (Isa. 44:22; Mic. 4:10); He redeemed David from his enemies (Ps. 69:18); He redeems His people from Sheol (Ps. 103:4); He redeems Israel in the tribulation (Isa. 43:1); He redeems through the death of Christ (Job 19:25; Isa. 52:3).[19]

Naomi's reference to Boaz as *gō'ēl* indicates Boaz would fulfill his obligations as kinsman-redeemer according to the Mosaic Law. In his function as kinsman-redeemer, Boaz became a type of Jesus Christ who is our kinsman-redeemer (see discussion under "Purpose" in the Introduction).

---

[19]See Helmer Ringgren, "גָּאַל," *Theological Dictionary*, vol. 2, pp. 350–55; R. Laird Harris, "גָּאַל," *Theological Wordbook*, vol. 1, pp. 144–45; A. R. Johnson, "The Primary Meaning of the Root גאל, *Vestus Testamentum* (Supplement), 1 (1953), pp. 67–77.

2. Benefit of Ruth (2:21–23)

Ruth is once more identified as "the Moabitess," a reminder that unusual blessing was about to come on one who was a foreigner. In further explaining to her mother-in-law Ruth told Naomi of Boaz' concern for her physical well-being and how he exhorted her to stay with his workers until they had finished the harvest. The protective care of Boaz is seen in his emphasis: "Stay with *my* workers until they finish harvesting all *my* grain" (v. 21). Boaz may also have suggested that Ruth remain with his workers until they had completed the wheat harvest, which was one month later (cf. v. 23).

Naomi indicated her complete satisfaction at Boaz' care for Ruth and therefore suggested that Ruth remain with Boaz' girls (v. 22). There was a danger that Ruth would be harmed if she would venture into someone else's field to glean without the company of the women who worked for Boaz. The phrase, "you might be harmed" ("lest others fall upon you," NASB; [Heb. *pāga'*]) sometimes means to kill (Judg. 8:21; 15:12; 18:25), but here means a hostile encounter or molestation. Naomi's concern was that Ruth remain with Boaz' workers to avoid being harmed.

Ruth followed the advice of Naomi and remained with the servant girls of Boaz for the duration of the barley and wheat harvest (2:23). Harvesting barley began the harvesting season (2 Sam. 21:9), with the entire harvest season lasting seven weeks, culminating in the Feast of Weeks (Lev. 23:15–21; Deut. 16:9–12).

The concluding statement of verse 23 is a reminder of Ruth's loyalty and faithfulness to her mother-in-law (cf. 1:16). Although Ruth harvested each day with the servant girls of Boaz, she did not live with them, rather, each evening she would return to the home of Naomi.

For Further Study

1. Read an article on kinsman-redeemer in a Bible dictionary or encyclopedia.

2. Develop a character study of Boaz in this chapter. What admirable qualities are evident in his life?

3. Develop a concordance study of the word blessed or blessing. How does God bless His people? How has God blessed you?

4. Trace the faithfulness of God to Ruth and Naomi in chapter 2. Can you discern God's faithfulness to you?

Chapter 3

Request of Ruth
(Ruth 3:1–18)

Naomi's concern for Ruth becomes evident in this chapter as she endeavors to arrange for a husband for her daughter-in-law. At the advice of Naomi, Ruth confronts Boaz, requesting that he marry her in fulfillment of the law of the kinsman-redeemer. Boaz promises to marry her if the nearer kinsman-redeemer refuses.

A. Suggestion of Naomi (3:1–5)

1. *Preparatory counsel* (3:1–4)

Naomi counseled Ruth concerning the function of the kinsman-redeemer. Through the intervention of Boaz, two essential needs of Naomi would be remedied: 1) She had been forced to sell her property because of poverty. The kinsman-redeemer could restore the property to the family by purchasing it (Lev. 25:23–28); if the kinsman-redeemer failed to restore the land to the family, it would automatically revert to the family in the Year of Jubilee (Lev. 25:10, 13). Boaz stood in a position to restore Naomi's property to her. 2) The name of Elimelech, Naomi's deceased husband, could be perpetuated and an heir provided to take the place of Elimelech through Boaz's marriage to Ruth.

To encourage Ruth's possible marriage to Boaz, Naomi suggested, "My daughter, should I not try to find a home for you, where you will be well provided for?" (3:1). The word "home" ("rest," NASB, KJV; [mānôah]) is normally translated "rest" since the word has reference to the state or condition of rest. Hence, in verse 1 it means the *condition of rest* and security attained by marriage."[1] It is used similarly in 1:9.

The purpose of Naomi's counsel is seen in the last clause of verse 1: "where you may be well provided for." Ruth would face considerable hardship in the ancient world as a widow but marriage would resolve her dilemma.

In case Ruth missed the point, Naomi became specific. She had Boaz in mind as a husband for Ruth! He was their kinsman and could fulfill his obligation as a kinsman-redeemer by marrying her (v. 2). Moreover, he was known to Ruth since she had been harvesting with his maids. Naomi also reminded Ruth where she could find Boaz: he would be winnowing barley on the threshing floor in the evening. The threshing floor was usually located on an elevated, exposed site so the breeze could aid in the winnowing process. The westerly wind in Israel began to blow late afternoon until after sunset. The grain was separated from the husk by animal-drawn sledges being pulled across the grain, which was then thrown into the air with a wooden fork. The breeze blew the chaff away while the kernels of grain dropped to the threshing floor. After dark the grain needed to be guarded, therefore, it was possible that Boaz would remain at the threshing floor that evening to guard the grain. It would be an opportune moment for Ruth to meet him.

There is an interesting symmetry in verses 3–4. Four commands are given in verse 3, "wash . . . perfume . . . put on . . . go down," followed by a negative command, "don't let him know you are there." Four commands again follow in verse 4, "note . . . go . . . uncover . . . lie down."[2]

In preparation for her important meeting with Boaz, Ruth was instructed to wash and perfume herself, put on her best clothes, and go down to the threshing floor to meet Boaz. The procedure

---

[1]Brown, Driver, and Briggs, *Hebrew and English Lexicon*, p. 629.
[2]Campbell, *Ruth*, p. 120.

seems to have a parallel in Ezekiel 16:9–13 which describes a
bride preparing for marriage. The word "wash" may also be
translated "bath" as in 2 Samuel 11:2. After bathing it was common to anoint the body with olive oil (cf. 2 Sam. 12:20). In this
instance it involved perfumed oil. A perfumed anointing oil that
was sometimes used was myrrh, which was mixed with spices to
produce a fragrant aroma.

> It was used to perfume royal garments (Ps. 45:8), beds (Prov.
> 7:17; Song of Solomon 3:6), and the human body (Song of Sol-
> omon 1:13; 5:5). According to Esther 2:12, it was considered to
> have other beneficial cosmetic effects, since a six-month series of
> beauty treatments employing oil of myrrh was given candidates
> for queenship in the Persian court.[3]

Naomi further instructed Ruth to put on her best clothes. The
question arises whether Ruth in her poverty in fact had any
"best clothes." Since "clothes" actually appears in the singular it
may be best to understand this as the cape or outer garment as
many have suggested. The cape would protect Ruth from the
chill of the night as well as allow her to remain anonymous for as
long as she purposed.[4]

The fact that Ruth was to "go down" to the threshing floor
suggests that it was at a lower level than the town of Bethlehem,
although the threshing floor would still have been at a raised
level to catch the wind. Ruth, however, was not to make herself
known to Boaz until he had finished eating and drinking for that
would hinder her purpose in coming (cf. v. 9).

Ruth was further instructed to take notice of the place where
Boaz would lie down on the threshing floor (v. 4). Naomi instructed her to go to Boaz at night and "uncover his feet and lie
down." In guarding the grain, Boaz was sleeping on the threshing floor and had covered himself with his cloak against the chill

---

[3]Gus W. Van Beek, "Frankincense and Myrrh," in *The Biblical Archaeol-
ogist Reader*, eds. Edward F. Campbell Jr., and David Noel Freedman, vol. 2
(Missoula, Mont.: Scholars Press, p. 115).

[4]Joyce G. Baldwin, "Ruth," in *The New Bible Commentary: Revised* (Grand
Rapids: William B. Eerdmans Publishing Co., 1970), p. 281.

of the night. Ruth was to cover herself with the portion of Boaz' cloak that covered his feet. No doubt she took the servant's position in which the servant would lie diagonally at his master's feet. There are no sexual or immoral overtones intended in this account.[5] Ruth's act was symbolic in that she was requesting Boaz to fulfill his duty as kinsman-redeemer and marry her. It is evident from 4:5 that Boaz understood Ruth's action as a request for marriage.

The final statement, "He will tell you what to do," suggests that Ruth was to await word from Boaz whether he would actually become the kinsman-redeemer by marrying her. Ruth's question was initially answered in 3:11–13 and finally in 4:10.

2. *Patient confidence* (3:5)

Ruth's submission and obedience to her mother-in-law is once again evident; she continues in the vein of her earlier promise (1:16–17). In a humble spirit Ruth quietly obeys Naomi in promising to follow her suggestion.

B. Supplication of Ruth (3:6–13)

1. *Request for marriage* (3:6–9)

The initial statement of 3:6 is a summary statement explaining that Ruth did everything that Naomi told her to do. The following verses provide the details. Ruth went down to the threshing floor—again a reminder that the village was located on a hill while the threshing floor, though on an elevated level, was on a lower level than the village. According to Naomi's instruction,

---

[5]It is unfortunate that Campbell suggests a possible sexual encounter took place on the threshing floor when the context militates against that view (cf. Campbell, *Ruth*, pp. 121, 130–31). Although he argues that "uncover his feet" is a euphemism for sexual relations, a lexical study of *gālâ* indicates it is not so used in this context; cf. Hans-Jürgen Zobel, "גָּלָה," *Theological Dictionary*, vol. 2, p. 479; Brown, Driver, and Briggs, *Hebrew and English Lexicon*, p. 163. Bullinger also suggests the phrase "spread the corner of your garment over me" (3:9) is a euphemism meaning "receive me in the way of marriage," *Figures of Speech*, p. 685.

Ruth observed where Boaz lay down and remained hidden until the appropriate moment.

Ruth waited until Boaz had finished eating and drinking. The ensuing phrase may explain why—he was in good spirits. Esther similarly waited until the king had eaten before she made her request (Esth. 7:2). The phrase "was in good spirits" ("his heart was merry," NASB) need not suggest overindulgence but is most likely associated with the joy that was prevalent in the harvest (cf. Isa. 9:3). The expression is sometimes used to denote the state of drunkenness but the statement is usually qualified. The phrase is used in 1 Samuel 25:36 of Nabal but it is also stated that he was "very drunk." Similarly 2 Samuel 13:28 indicates Amnon in high spirits "from drinking wine." The expression, however, is a normal reference to the joy of the people (1 Kings 8:66; Prov. 15:15). The context of Ruth 3:7 does not suggest drunkenness; hence, it is best to understand the statement as expressing the joy that Boaz felt during harvest time.

Having eaten, Boaz went "to lie down at the far end of the grain pile" (3:7). Boaz followed the common custom of guarding the grain as the people normally did until the harvest was over; thus, Boaz lay down at the end of the sheaves of grain. It is evident from verse 8 that Ruth waited until Boaz was asleep; then she uncovered his feet and lay down. In the middle of the night Boaz was startled (Heb. *hārad;* the same word describes the fear of Saul upon seeing the Philistines in preparation for battle). As he turned (Heb. *lāpat;* the word may also mean grasp or grope—the word is so used in Judges 16:29 of Samson grasping the pillars of the Philistine temple) or reached forward he discovered a woman lying at his feet.

Unable to see the identity of the person, Boaz called out, "Who are you?" (3:9). Ruth responded and identified herself, "I am your servant Ruth." Ruth assumed a servile position in referring to herself as a servant (Heb. *'āmâ*), a term used to depict literal slaves (cf. Gen. 20:17; Exod. 2:5). Here the reference is used figuratively, but it indicates that Ruth's request originates from one in a humble position.

The purpose of Ruth's visit is made clear in her petition: "Spread the corner of your garment over me, since you are a kinsman-redeemer." Because Boaz was a near relative and as such, a kinsman-redeemer, Ruth was requesting protection through marriage. That the expression "spread the corner of your garment over me" indicates a request for marriage is seen in other Old Testament passages. A similar phrase is used for marriage in Deuteronomy 22:30, "he must not dishonor his father's bed" ("he shall not uncover his father's skirt," NASB; cf. Deut. 27:20). Ezekiel 16:8 is particularly clear in this usage in describing the covenant of marriage between the Lord and the nation Israel. The symbol of spreading a garment over a widow was a common indication of claiming a widow in marriage as attested by Tabari's commentary:

> In the Jahiliya, when a man's father or brother or son died and left a widow, the dead man's heir, if he came at once and threw his garment over her, had the right to marry her under the dowry of (i.e. already paid by) her (deceased) lord, or to give her in marriage and take her dowry. But if she anticipated him and went off to her own people, then the disposal of her hand belonged to herself.[6]

That this was a common symbol of marriage, not only among Jews and Arabs, but also Hindus is observed in the century-old commentary by Jamieson:

> To spread a skirt over one is, in the East, a symbolical action denoting protection. To this day in many parts of the East to say of any one that he put his skirt over a woman is synonymous with saying that he married her; and at all the marriages of the modern Jews and Hindoos one part of the ceremony is for the bridegroom to put a silken or cotton cloak around his bride.[7]

---

[6]G. A. Cooke, "The Book of Ruth," in *The Cambridge Bible for Schools and Colleges* (Cambridge: University Press, 1918), p. 11.

[7]Jamieson, *Ruth*, p. 132. Some manuscripts have the plural form for garment in which case it may have reference to wings as in 2:12. Ruth has come to Israel in faith under the protection of Yahweh's wings and now seeks protection through marriage under Boaz' wings.

2. *Assurance of marriage* (3:10–13)

Boaz immediately recognized the faithfulness of Ruth in her quest to maintain the name of her deceased husband through marriage to her near relative—even though he was an older man. Boaz invoked a prayer of blessing on Ruth for her faithfulness (see discussion on "blessed" under 2:20). He suggested that this act of kindness was greater than the kindness that she had shown earlier (see discussion on kindness under 1:8). Her earlier kindness was that shown to Naomi in which she remained with her mother-in-law (1:16–17) and provided for her needs (2:18). Now, however, Ruth refused to follow her own desires in seeking a younger man for a husband but sought instead to continue the name of her deceased husband through a levirite marriage, even at the cost of marrying an older man. It is possible that Ruth had received marriage proposals,[8] but rejected them, caring neither for the rich nor poor young men but was intent only on fulfilling her obligation to her dead husband. The definite article suggests specific young men, perhaps those who harvested Boaz' crops, or other prominent young men from the village.

Having first commended Ruth for her loyalty, Boaz now answered her request (3:11). He sought to allay Ruth's concern in telling her, "And now, my daughter, don't be afraid. I will do for you all you ask." His response seemed like a heaven-sent answer since Naomi had earlier reminded Ruth, "He will tell you what to do" (3:4). In his answer Boaz agreed to fulfill his obligation as kinsman-redeemer and marry Ruth. Boaz was not at all reluctant to marry Ruth since all his fellow townsmen knew that Ruth was a woman of noble character. The phrase, "all my fellow townsmen" is literally "all the gate of my people." The gate denotes the prominent place at the entrance of the city where the caravans stopped and carried out their business, where legal transactions took place, and where local gossip was disseminated (cf. Gen. 23:10; 34:20; Job 29:7; Prov. 31:23; Amos 5:12, 15). No

---

[8]Campbell, *Ruth*, p. 124.

doubt Ruth had been a common topic of conversation since she was a foreigner. Yet the concensus of the people was that Ruth was a woman of noble character (Heb. *ḥayil*). The term (which is used in a compound form of Boaz in 2:1) has a basic meaning of strength and power and in this passage means *"do worthily, efficiently"* and usually involves moral worth.[9] It is used of a woman in Proverbs 12:4 and 31:10. The context of Proverbs 31:10 indicates a woman with this characteristic was efficient and hard working as well as being a woman of strength and dignity (cf. 31:25). Boaz' statement vindicates the moral integrity of Ruth.

In his response Boaz acknowledged that he was a near relative and also expressed his willingness to be a kinsman-redeemer to Ruth; however there was one who was a nearer relative. To him fell the responsibility of kinsman-redeemer since he had a prior claim. Boaz recognized both the legitimacy of Ruth's claim as well as the social rectitude in which the matter had to be carried out, hence he reminded her of the one who had a prior claim.

> This claim is often jealously guarded by first cousins in marriage among the Arabs. This declaration surely absolves Boaz from improper relations with Ruth since, if the other kinsman had accepted, his own good name and hers among his own kin would have been irrevocably damaged and perhaps their lives forfeited.[10]

Since Ruth's purpose in coming had been resolved she might have been tempted to leave, therefore, Boaz told her, "Stay here for the night" (v. 13). It would have been dangerous for Ruth to attempt to return to the city at night because of thieves or immoral men (cf. Song of Songs 5:7).

In the morning Boaz determined to follow the proper procedure in providing for the two widows. If the near relative would agree to marry Ruth, good; however, if he did not wish to redeem her then Boaz would most certainly do it. It appears from

---

[9]Brown, Driver, and Briggs, *Hebrew and English Lexicon*, p. 298.
[10]Gray, *Ruth*, p. 419.

Deuteronomy 25:7–10 that the nearest relative would be encouraged to be the redeemer; however, he probably had the freedom to reject the opportunity—although not without public scandal.

Boaz confirmed his intention to redeem Ruth with the oath, "as surely as the LORD lives." This oath formula is used some thirty times in Judges, Samuel, and Kings (cf. 2 Sam. 3:55; 15:21; 2 Kings 5:20) and means "as sure as Yahweh is the living God, you can count on what I promise."[11] Having reassured Ruth, Boaz told her to "Lie here until morning" when he would carry out his promise to her.

C. Security of Ruth (3:14–18)

1. *Generosity of Boaz* (3:14–17)

At Boaz' suggestion Ruth remained at Boaz' feet until morning, but before anyone could be recognized Ruth got up and left the threshing floor. Since women began their work early Ruth would not have been conspicuous at that hour; furthermore, it was sufficiently early so that no one could be recognized. Although nothing immoral had occurred at the threshing floor, rumors could quickly turn the innocent event into a public scandal. Ruth apparently left the threshing floor before daybreak at the suggestion of Boaz, although the statement, "he said," should probably be translated "he thought," or "he said to himself" (cf. Gen. 20:11). In his own mind Boaz was concerned that no one would find out that a woman had come to the threshing floor. The news would most certainly ruin both of them.

Before Ruth left the threshing floor Boaz told her, "Bring me the shawl you are wearing and hold it out" (v. 15). Shawl (Heb. *mitpaḥat*) comes from a root word meaning "to spread" (cf. Isa. 3:22) and may denote the long, narrow head shawl seen on the women in Sennacherib's wall relief of the capture of Lachish.[12] Another possibility is that the word is a synonym for the cloak

---

[11]Campbell, *Ruth*, p. 126.
[12]Campbell, *Ruth*. See Illustration 4 and discussion on page 127.

("best clothes," NIV) mentioned in 3:3. In any case the shawl had to be of sufficient strength to carry the weight of the barley.

Boaz told Ruth to get a good grip of the shawl as he measured out six measures of barley into it. The explanation concerning the barley is mentioned in verse 17—it was a gift for Naomi. Although the actual measure is not given, it could not have been the ephah mentioned in 2:17 since that would have amounted to several hundred pounds and would have been impossible for Ruth to carry. Two other possibilities exist. It could have been an omer (1/10 ephah), which was approximately two quarts. The gift would then have been about twelve quarts of barley, actually a small gift. More than likely the measure was the seah, which was 1/3 of an ephah. Six measures would have been about ninety pounds—certainly heavy for a woman, but possible. That this was probably the measure is further seen in the statement, "(he) put it on her," suggesting that Boaz helped load the barley on her head, which would have been the normal way she would have carried the barley into the city. "The gift is intended for Naomi, who would have to consent to the marriage, as standing in the relation of parent to Ruth."[13] Having received the gift, Ruth returned to Bethlehem.[14]

When Ruth returned home, Naomi asked, "How did it go, my daughter?" (v. 16), literally, "Who are you?" The question was not asked because of prevailing darkness but rather inquired, "In what condition did you come?" or "How did you fare?" (cf. Gen. 27:18). Ruth's response indicates that this is the sense of the question. Naomi had advised Ruth concerning this important mission; she had much interest in how the matter had turned out.

Ruth told Naomi of Boaz' promise at the threshing floor (vv. 10–13) and gave her the barley with the explanation from Boaz, "Don't go back to your mother-in-law empty-handed" (v. 17).

---

[13]Cooke, *Ruth*, p. 12.
[14]There is a textual problem in the phrase, "he went back to town." The Masoretic text reads "he" while some Hebrew mss., the Vulgate and the Syriac read "she." The passage makes it clear Ruth is meant—Boaz went later (4:1).

There is a definite emphasis on the word empty-handed since it is the same word mentioned in 1:21. Upon her return from Moab Naomi was bitter; the Lord had brought her back to Judah empty—without husband or sons. In the development of chapter 3 there is the clear indication that she would no longer be empty. The provision of barley was but the foreshadowing of the fullness to which Naomi would come. Chapter 4 will see the fruition of Naomi's fullness in the birth of a son to Ruth, who would become the grandfather of David and the ancestor of Christ.

2. *Justice of Boaz* (3:18)

Having heard Ruth recount the details of her visit with Boaz, Naomi instructed her to remain quietly at home until the matter was resolved (v. 18). The first statement, "until you find out what happens" (i.e., who would be the kinsman-redeemer, Boaz or the nearer relative) seems to emphasize the sovereign outworking of God's purpose in the matter and all that Ruth could do would be to wait for the plan of God to be consummated. The latter statement, "The man will not rest until the matter is settled today" indicates the determined initiative Boaz would take to see that the matter was resolved. It also indicates the intimate interest of Boaz in Ruth's redemption and it seems to anticipate the nearer relative's rejection. The final segment of this historical drama is nearing it fulfillment!

For Further Study

1. Analyze and evaluate the actions of Naomi in chapter 2.

2. Study the "noble character" of Ruth as seen in this chapter (cf. 2:11).

3. Read an article on marriage in a Bible dictionary or encyclopedia.

4. How is the wisdom of Boaz reflected in this chapter?

Chapter 4

Redemption of Ruth
(Ruth 4:1–22)

The drama of the Book of Ruth climaxes in this chapter as Boaz confronts the near kinsman-redeemer concerning the redemption of Naomi's land. When he discovers he must also marry Ruth if he is to fulfill his role of redemption, he renounces his right to be the kinsman-redeemer. Since Boaz is next in line, he announces his intention to be the kinsman-redeemer before the town witnesses. He marries Ruth and a son is born of the union. The child becomes the grandfather of David, Israel's great king, out of whose lineage comes Jesus who is the Savior of the world and Israel's Messiah.

A. Discussion concerning Ruth (4:1–6)

1. *Request to redeem* (4:1–4)

In order to initiate the proceedings effecting the redemption of Ruth, Boaz went up to the town gate. This was a large open space near the entrance of the city where business and legal matters were conducted (see also under 3:11). Since many of the townspeople worked outside the city during the day the area at the entrance to the city was a convenient place to conduct business because the people passed by there each day. It was at the city gate that Abraham purchased a burial place for Sarah (Gen. 23:10ff.); Absalom influenced people by speaking to them at the gate (2 Sam. 15:2). Even kings sat at the entrance to the city (1 Kings 22:10; Jer. 38:7). Justice was also administered at the city gate. One guilty of manslaughter presented his case before elders before he could enter the city (Josh. 20:4). Criminal acts were discussed and judgment was rendered at the gate (Deut. 21:18–21). Hence, it was at the gate that Boaz presented his case before the elders of the town.

Soon the kinsman-redeemer came along and Boaz summoned him to sit down. It is unclear whether the man knew that Boaz was holding a hearing on the matter. The statement "my friend" suggests Boaz actually knew his name since the Hebrew wording is an approximation of the English "Mr. So-and-so." The man responded and joined Boaz in the hearing at the gate.

Boaz summoned ten elders from the town to act as witnesses in the proceedings (4:2). Elders were the heads of leading families but were also probably selected on the basis of their age since the term (Heb. *zāqēn*) denotes an aged man. The term is also related to the verb *zāqān*, meaning "beard." The elders served as judges, dealing with criminal charges (Deut. 21:18–21), but also dealt with family matters such as the fulfillment of the Levirate marriage (Deut. 25:7–9).

The selection of ten elders is significant. Later in Israel's history a minimum of ten men was required for synagogue worship as well as the quorum necessary for the marriage benediction.[1]

Boaz explained the problem to the kinsman-redeemer. Having returned from Moab, Naomi was forced to sell the piece of land that belonged to her deceased husband, Elimelech (4:3). The verb "is selling" is in the perfect tense in the Hebrew text, which normally denotes completed action and therefore could read "sold." The information in verses 5 and 9 indicates, however, that she was in the process of selling the land and therefore emphasized her determination or resolve to sell the land. Although Naomi had owned the land she apparently had not

---

[1]Smith, *Interpreter's Bible*, vol. 2, p. 847.

realized any income from it and now, in her poverty, she was forced to sell the land.[2]

In the redemption of the land it was offered to the nearest relative first (Jer. 32:6–12) and for this reason Boaz informed the kinsman-redeemer (4:4). The redemption of the land was important since it assured that the land would remain in the family; moreover, it was the responsibility of the kinsman-redeemer to redeem the land for the poor relative (Lev. 25:25). As indicated in this verse, the kinsman-redeemer determined whether the land remained in the family or not; should he decide not to redeem, then the land could pass to someone outside the family. In that case the original owner would gain possession of the land in the Year of Jubilee (Lev. 25:28). In this incident Boaz exhorted the kinsman-redeemer to decide whether or not he would redeem in the presence of witnesses, making the event a legal matter. He had the option since he was the nearest relative; however, Boaz reminded him that he was next in line. The kinsman-redeemer responded, "I will redeem it."

2. *Refusal to redeem* (4:5–6)

It is evident that Boaz was eager to marry Ruth, yet he could not openly display his intentions and for this reason he mentioned the acquisition of the land first. Now, however, he reminded the kinsman-redeemer of a further obligation if he would fulfill his function as the kinsman-redeemer: he had to acquire Ruth the Moabitess as his wife to maintain the name of the deceased man.[3]

Although it is generally assumed Boaz' statement refers to the

---

[2]The problem of whether a widow could or could not own property is not entirely clear. Although Numbers 27:8–11 does not mention a widow inheriting land it is nonetheless an argument from silence and does not answer all the variables. For the suggestion that a widow could hold property see Paulus Cassel, "The Book of Ruth," in *Lange's Commentary on the Holy Scriptures* (Grand Rapids: Zondervan Publishing House, 1960 reprint), p. 46.

[3]There is a textual problem with the Masoretic text reading, "buy the land from Naomi and from Ruth" while the Vulgate and Syriac read, "Naomi, you acquire Ruth the Moabitess." The latter reading is also supported by v. 10.

levirate law of Deuteronomy 25:5-10 that appears unlikely. Several factors are involved in the passage: 1) Only when brothers were living together and one of them died was the other brother to be the kinsman-redeemer. 2) The obligation relates specifically to brothers but does not comment on more distant relatives. 3) The levirate law was in effect only when no son had been born to the deceased person. The reason for this is clear since it was the first-born son who received the inheritance and became the patriarchal leader, in effect, replacing the deceased father. In that sense the primary purpose of the levirate law would be fulfilled: "that his name will not be blotted out from Israel" (Deut. 25:6). The deceased man's lineage would be perpetuated through the birth of a son to his widow. In addition, Craigie suggests that the deceased man could share in the covenant promises of God through those he left behind him since the promises were "to you and your descendants after you" (Gen. 17:7-9).[4]

Since Deuteronomy 25 does not strictly apply to this event, it indicates "a period or a *milieu* in which the law of levirate was a matter for the clan rather than for the family in the strict sense."[5]

When the kinsman-redeemer discovered that the redemption of the land also involved marriage to Ruth the Moabitess he declined (4:6). The indication appears to be that he would have been prepared to purchase the field *or* marry Ruth, but not both. The man stated emphatically, "Then I cannot redeem it because I might endanger my own estate." Although there is no indication whether or not he was wealthy, it appears he was not since the purchase of the land would have endangered his own estate. Had the man purchased the land without marrying Ruth, the land would have become part of his estate; however, if he

---

[4] P. C. Craigie, *The Book of Deuteronomy* in *The New International Commentary on the Old Testament* (Grand Rapids: William B. Eerdmans Publishing Co., 1976), p. 314.

[5] Roland de Vaux, *Ancient Israel* (New York: McGraw-Hill Book Company, 1965), p. 38.

also married Ruth and a son was born of the union, the son would receive the land as his inheritance and the estate of the kinsman-redeemer would be reduced by the amount he paid for the field. Hence, his own estate would be in jeopardy if he were not a wealthy man.

In his response the kinsman-redeemer made his own position clear; twice he mentioned that he could not redeem the property, stating emphatically, "*You* redeem it *yourself.*" The story points ahead to the necessity of Boaz becoming the kinsman-redeemer; the sovereign purpose of God would be fulfilled through Boaz.

B. Requisition of Ruth (4:7–12)

1. *Transfer of land* (4:7–8)

The writer describes the earlier symbolic custom in the redemption and transfer of property that was no longer in vogue when the book was written. The kinsman-redeemer indicated that he was renouncing his right to redeem the land by the symbolic action in which he removed his sandal and gave it to the one who would be the kinsman-redeemer. The action was carried out in the presence of witnesses before whom the kinsman-redeemer was indicating that he was forfeiting his right of redemption.[6] In this case it was not a question of whether Ruth would be redeemed but rather by whom. In Deuteronomy 25:8–10 the case is different in that the refusal of the kinsman-redeemer meant the deceased man's name would not be perpetuated since there was no other redeemer. It was for this reason that the widow would ceremoniously spit in the face of the one who refused to redeem.

The custom of the transfer of the sandal was probably derived from the fact that property was assumed by walking on it. For example, God's promise of Canaan to Joshua was confirmed by the promise that he would possess all the land on which he walked (Josh. 1:3; cf. Deut. 11:24). Similarly, having promised

---

[6]de Vaux, *Ancient Israel*, pp. 38, 169.

Abraham the land of Canaan, God invited him to walk on the land symbolizing that his posterity would one day possess the land (Gen. 13:17).

In this case the near kinsman-redeemer legalized his relinquishing of the right of kinsman-redeemer through the presence of witnesses as he removed his sandal and gave it to Boaz.

2. Testimony of Witnesses (4:9–12)

After the near kinsman-redeemer declined to redeem, Boaz announced his twofold intention in the presence of the elders and all the people: he would acquire the land (v. 9) and marry Ruth (v. 10). Although Boaz had originally summoned ten elders (v. 2), a number of people had gathered by now—who also became witnesses in the legal scene.[7] This is emphasized in verse 11 where the people acknowledge that they are witnesses to the event. Since very little was recorded in those days and since there is no indication that anything was recorded in this transaction, a crowd of reliable witnesses would have been very important.[8]

Boaz affirmed in the presence of the witnesses that he was assuming from Naomi the property that had belonged to Elimelech, Kilion, and Mahlon, and he did this to prevent the land from passing outside of the family.[9] Evidently, the inheritance of Kilion and Mahlon had passed to Naomi rather than their widows when they died.

In addition to acquiring the property, Boaz had also acquired Ruth the Moabitess, Mahlon's widow (4:10). The word also (Heb. *gam*) places a greater emphasis on what follows—namely, Boaz was emphasizing the fact that he had also acquired Ruth as his wife.[10] This is further seen in the emphatic statement "I have acquired *to me*" (Heb. *qānītī lī*) whereas the statement in verse 9

---

[7]Campbell, *Ruth*, p. 151.

[8]Cundall and Morris, *Judges and Ruth*, p. 308.

[9]The Hebrew term *qānâ* is translated "bought" in v. 9 and "acquired" in v. 10. The sense of acquired is correct.

[10]Brown, Driver, and Briggs, *Hebrew and English Lexicon*, p. 169.

simply reads "I have bought" (Heb. *qānîtî*). The text again emphasizes that Ruth was a Moabitess; she was also the widow of Mahlon. This had not been indicated previously (cf. 1:2–5).

Boaz explained the purpose for which he had acquired Ruth as his wife: "in order to maintain the name of the dead with his property, so that his name will not disappear from among his family or from the town records." Through Boaz' marriage to Ruth and the subsequent birth of a son, the child would be considered the son of Elimelech and thus the name of the dead would be perpetuated. The reference to the town records is literally, "the gate of his place," referring to the town gate that was the hub of business and social life. Once more the emphasis is on the continuance of the man's name in the community.

The elders as well as the people at the gate affirmed their witness to the betrothal of Boaz to Ruth and in addition to giving their legal affirmation they also pronounced a blessing on them. Their prayer was that the offspring of Boaz and Ruth would be as numerous as those of Rachel and Leah (4:11). The two women were the wives of Jacob and together with their maidservants brought forth twelve sons from whom the entire nation of Israel evolved. Rachel was the mother of Joseph (Gen. 30:22, 24) and Benjamin (Gen. 35:18), while Leah was the mother of Reuben, Simeon, Levi, Judah, Issachar, Zebulun, and Dinah (Gen. 29:31–35; 30:17–21). The mention of Rachel and Leah is significant since both were revered among the people of Bethlehem, for Rachel's tomb was nearby (Gen. 35:19–20), and since Bethlehem was in Judah they were descendants of Leah through Judah (Gen. 29:35).

The final statement of verse 11 is a form of Hebrew poetry called synonymous parallelism in which the second clause repeats the thought of the first clause in different words, thus "have standing in Ephrathah" parallels "be famous in Bethlehem." The word standing (Heb. *ḥayil;* NASB, "wealth") here means "do worthily, efficiently"[11] (see discussion under 2:1

---

[11]Brown, Driver, and Briggs, *Hebrew and English Lexicon,* p. 298.

and 3:11), no doubt in the sense of a large posterity. Famous (Heb. *qārā*) means "to call a name" and is a prayer that Boaz would be renowned through his posterity, thus, "Make to thyself a well-established name through thy marriage with Ruth, by a host of worthy sons who shall make thy name renowned."[12]

Whereas the people expressed their hope that Ruth might bear many children (v. 11), they now prayed that the posterity of Boaz would be like that of Perez who was born to Tamar by Judah (Gen. 38:29). Tamar is mentioned because there is a decided parallel between Tamar who was a widow and had a child by an older man and Ruth who was also a widow and now marrying an older man. Moreover, Perez was the ancestor of Boaz (1 Chron. 2:4–11). Yet there was also the solemn recognition that the Lord was the giver of life; only through the gracious gift of God would they be assured of a prolific posterity (cf. 1 Sam. 2:20).

C. Marriage of Ruth (4:13–17)

1. *Birth* (4:13)

When the legal proceedings were over, Boaz took Ruth and she became his wife. The NIV omits the phrase, "and he went in to her," suggestive both of Boaz entering the woman's chamber of the tent (cf. Gen. 31:33), as well as sexual relations. The statement, "the LORD enabled her to conceive" completes the thought initiated in verse 12, which indicates that the Lord was now fulfilling the wish of the people and giving Ruth a child. Through the Lord's blessing a child was born to Boaz and Ruth through whose seed David and ultimately Christ would come. Just as the son born to Ruth was a gift of God in Ruth's redemption, so Christ was also the gift of God for the redemption of the world (John 3:16).

2. *Blessing* (4:14–17)

In the excitement of the birth of a son to Ruth the women of Bethlehem came to Naomi, expressing their joy: "Praise be to

---

[12]Keil and Delitzsch, *Joshua, Judges, Ruth*, p. 491.

the LORD, who this day has not left you without a kinsman-redeemer" (4:14). There is an obvious contrast to the words of the women as they first saw Naomi upon her return from Moab (1:19). In their delight the women ascribe the joyful event to the sovereign work of the Lord; He was the one who brought about this wonderful event. The ascription of blessing to God finds expression in the Eighteen Benedictions that later formed a part of the regular synagogue worship. The phrase, "Blessed art Thou, O LORD" was an intrinsic part of the statements, hence their name.[13]

The women blessed the name of God for not having left Naomi without a kinsman-redeemer. Although Boaz was the kinsman-redeemer, the reference here is to the newborn child.

> This redeemer was not Boaz, but the son just born. They called him a redeemer of Naomi, not because he would one day redeem the whole of Naomi's possessions, but because as the son of Ruth he was also the son of Naomi (ver. 17), and as such would take away the reproach of childlessness from her, would comfort her, and tend her in her old age, and thereby become her true *goël*, i.e. her deliverer.[14]

"May he become famous throughout Israel!" exclaimed the women. Famous (Heb. *qārā*) literally means "to call" and expresses the desire that the child would one day be well known throughout Israel. Perhaps it was a "wish for children who will be reckoned as his descendants."[15]

The women recognized the ultimate blessing that would come to Naomi through her grandson: "He will renew your life and sustain you in your old age" (4:15). Renew (Heb. *shûb*) is the ordinary word for return and no doubt there is a play on words here as Naomi, the one who returned to the land destitute,

---

[13]Westcott has a valuable, extended discussion on the subject of blessing; in addition, he recites the Eighteen Benedictions (B. F. Westcott, *The Epistle to the Hebrews*, Grand Rapids: William B. Eerdmans Publishing Co., 1965 reprint), pp. 203–10. See also discussion under 2:19.

[14]Keil and Delitzsch, *Joshua, Judges, Ruth*, p. 492.

[15]Smith, *Interpreter's Bible*, vol. 2, p. 850.

would now experience her life returning to her in joy (cf. 1:21).[16] Now Naomi could look forward to her old age with joy, knowing that the child would become her provider. The word sustain (Heb. *kûl*) means to provide with food. It is used in Genesis 45:11 where Joseph promised to provide food for his brothers in the remaining years of famine; in 50:21, following the death of Jacob, Joseph reaffirmed his promises as the physical provider for his brothers (cf. 2 Sam. 19:32–33; 20:3).

Naomi could be at ease concerning her old age because a boy had been born to her daughter-in-law who loved her. Ruth had displayed a consistent loyalty and love toward her mother-in-law; she had forsaken her native Moab to be with Naomi (1:16), and she had provided for Naomi upon arriving in the land (2:18, 23). As a result, Naomi could be certain that Ruth would continue to provide for her mother-in-law through her son who had been born. Ruth was of more value to Naomi than seven sons. The statement reinforces Ruth's devotion of Naomi for seven is the number of perfection and seven sons were considered the ideal family blessed by God (cf. 1 Sam. 2:5; Job 1:2; Jer. 15:9; 1 Chron. 2:15).

In her delight Naomi "took the child, laid him in her lap and cared for him" (4:16). Some see in this a formal act of adoption[17]; however, there is no clear evidence of adoption in the Old Testament. Moreover, this would not be adoption in the strict sense since the so-called adoption takes place within the family and in the direct line.[18] The reference to Naomi caring for the child (lit. "became his nurse") does not refer to wet-nursing but rather it means Naomi became his guardian.[19]

The women continue to play an important part in the story as they exclaimed, "Naomi has a son" (4:17). Since Boaz was the

---

[16]"It is no coincidence that the story-teller here uses, in its causative form, the verb 'return' which dominated the scene along the road back from Moab in 1:6–22; note that the only other causative of *šûb* is in Naomi's complaint in 1:21" (Campbell, *Ruth*, p. 168).

[17]Kennedy, *Ruth*, p. 61.

[18]de Vaux, *Ancient Israel*, p. 51.

[19]Campbell, *Ruth*, pp. 164–65.

kinsman-redeemer in redeeming all that belonged to Elimelech (4:9), and since he had married Ruth, the daughter-in-law of Naomi, it could be said, "Naomi has a son."

It is unusual that the women named the child;[20] there may have been social factors involved of which we are unaware today. They gave him the name Obed which means "servant," perhaps suggestive of his role of caring for Naomi in her old age. The name is not frequently found in the Old Testament; on occasion it is used in combination with deity such as the name of Obadiah, meaning "servant of the Lord."

An important concluding point is immediately made, linking Obed as the ancestor of Jesse and David. The emphasis is clear and points to the note on which the book will terminate—descending from Obed was David, Israel's great king.

D. Posterity of Ruth (4:18–22)

The genealogy forms a fitting conclusion to the book and is not a later addition, but an integral part of the book. The opening statement, "This, then, is the family line of Perez," is similar to the introductory formulas found in the genealogical tables (cf. Gen. 5:1; 6:9; 10:1) and also similar to the chronology of 1 Chronicles 2:4–13. Since the chronology from Perez to David covers about eight hundred years it appears there are omissions in the chronology.[21]

Perez was the son of Judah by Tamar (Gen. 38:12–30). Hezron, who was among the family of Jacob that went down to Egypt (Gen. 46:12), fathered Ram who is mentioned in 1 Chronicles 2:9 but is otherwise unknown. Amminadab, the father-in-law of Aaron (Exod. 6:23), fathered Nahshon who is mentioned as the head of the house of Judah (Num. 1:7; 7:12; 10:14). Salmon (also known as Salmah or Salma) was the husband of Rahab of whom

---

[20]The grammar is difficult at this point. Some suggest the name the women actually gave is omitted at this point since the text simply reads, "the women called to him a name."

[21]See J. B. Payne, "Chronology of the Old Testament," ZPEB, vol. 1, pp. 829–45.

was born Boaz. Jesse was the wealthy Bethlehemite landowner and father of David (1 Sam. 17:12). He is mentioned in the messianic prophecies as being the ancestor from whose lineage a Branch would come forth, the Messiah, who would rule the nation (Isa. 11:1, 10). David was Israel's great king who unified the nation, made Jerusalem the religious and political capital, vastly expanded Israel's borders through successful warfare, and brought prosperity to the nation. To David was given the unconditional Davidic covenant (2 Sam. 7:12–16) in which David's greater son, the Messiah, was promised an everlasting throne and kingdom.[22]

The structure of the genealogy is significant:

> It is also worthy of notice that the whole chain from *Perez* to *David* consists of ten links, five of which (from Perez to Nahshon) belong to the 430 years of the sojourn in Egypt, and five (from Salmon to David) to the 476 years between the exodus from Egypt and the death of David. This symmetrical division is apparently as intentional as the limitation of the whole genealogy to ten members, for the purpose of stamping upon it through the number ten as the seal of completeness the character of a perfect, concluded, and symmetrical whole.[23]

But the ultimate purpose for the genealogy was to draw attention to David and ultimately David's greater son, Jesus Christ. It is noteworthy that this genealogy is also found in Matthew 1, which draws attention to the Davidic origin of Jesus Christ (Matt. 1:1). Thus the Book of Ruth shines forth during the dark, depraved period of the judges, anticipating a day when a redeemer from the line of David would come forth as the kinsman-redeemer of all humanity.

For Further Study

1. Read an article on David in a Bible encyclopedia or dictionary.

---

[22]See J. Dwight Pentecost, *Things To Come* (Grand Rapids: Zondervan Publishing House), pp. 100–15.

[23]Keil and Delitzsch, *Joshua, Judges, Ruth*, p. 493.

2. Study the disposition of Naomi in this chapter and contrast it with chapter 1. How do circumstances affect the Christian's disposition?

3. What can you learn from the Israelites who saw the sovereign hand of God in all events (cf. 4:14)?

4. Study the New Testament passages that depict Jesus Christ as the Redeemer of the world.

Bibliography

Aharoni, Yohanan. *The Land of the Bible.* Philadelphia: Westminster Press, 1967.

Baldwin, J. G. "Ruth," *The New Bible Commentary: Revised.* Grand Rapids: Eerdmans, 1970.

Botterweck, G. Johannes, and Ringgren, Helmer, eds. *Theological Dictionary of the Old Testament.* 4 vols. Grand Rapids: Eerdmans, 1977–1980.

Brown, Francis, Driver, S. R., and Briggs, Charles A. *A Hebrew and English Lexicon of the Old Testament.* Oxford: At the Clarendon Press, 1968.

Bullinger, E. W. *Figures of Speech Used in the Bible.* Grand Rapids: Baker, 1968 reprint.

Campbell, Edward F., Jr. *Ruth* in *The Anchor Bible.* Garden City, N. Y.: Doubleday, 1975.

Cassel, Paulus. "The Book of Ruth," *Lange's Commentary on the Holy Scriptures*, vol. 2. Grand Rapids: Zondervan, 1960 reprint.

Cooke, G. A. *The Book of Ruth.* Cambridge: University Press, 1918.

Cundall, Arthur E. and Morris, Leon. *Judges and Ruth.* Chicago: InterVarsity Press, 1968.

Davis, John J. *Conquest and Crisis: Studies in Joshua, Judges, and Ruth.* Grand Rapids: Baker, 1969.

73

de Vaux, Roland. *Ancient Israel.* New York: McGraw-Hill, 1965.

Douglas, J. D. *The New Bible Dictionary.* Grand Rapids: Eerdmans, 1962.

Finegan, Jack. *Light from the Ancient Past.* Princeton: Princeton University Press, 1959.

Gray, John. *Joshua, Judges and Ruth* in *The Century Bible.* Greenwood, S.C.: Attic Press, 1967.

Harris, R. Laird, Archer, Gleason L. Jr., and Waltke, Bruce K., eds. *Theological Wordbook of the Old Testament.* 2 vols. Chicago: Moody, 1980.

Jacob, Edmond. *Theology of the Old Testament.* New York: Harper & Row, 1958.

Jamieson, Robert, Fausset, A. R., and Brown, David. *A Commentary Critical, Experimental and Practical on the Old and New Testaments.* 6 vols. Grand Rapids: Eerdmans, 1945 reprint.

Kaiser, Walter C., Jr. *Toward an Old Testament Theology.* Grand Rapids: Zondervan, 1978.

Keil, C. F., and Delitzsch, F. *Joshua, Judges, Ruth* in *Biblical Commentary on the Old Testament.* Grand Rapids: Eerdmans, 1968 reprint.

Kennedy, A. R. S. *The Book of Ruth: The Hebrew Text with Grammatical Notes and Vocabulary.* London: Society for Promoting Christian Knowledge, 1928.

Knight, George A. F. *Ruth and Jonah* in *Torch Bible Commentaries.* London: SCM Press, 1950.

Payne, J. Barton, *The Theology of the Older Testament.* Grand Rapids: Zondervan, 1962.

Pfeiffer, Charles F. "Ruth," in *The Wycliffe Bible Commentary.* Chicago: Moody Press, 1962.

Ringgren, Helmer. *Israelite Religion.* Philadelphia: Fortress, 1966.

Smith, L. P. "The Book of Ruth," in *The Interpreter's Bible.* vol. 2. New York: Cokesbury, 1953.

Tenney, Merrill C., gen. ed. *The Zondervan Pictorial Encyclopedia of the Bible.* 5 vols. Grand Rapids: Zondervan, 1975.

Unger, Merrill F. *Archaeology and the Old Testament.* Grand Rapids: Zondervan, 1954.

Unger, Merrill F. and White, William, Jr. *Nelson's Expository Dictionary of the Old Testament.* Nashville: Thomas Nelson, 1980.